GW00675515

'This is an adventure.'
Steve Zissou

Aaron Turner

IGNI

A restaurant's first year

Photography by Julian Kingma

hardie grant books

the end

It all started with a restaurant called Loam, down the end of a dirt road, behind a small town, nestled on an olive grove overlooking the bay. It was simple, thirty or so seats, a small team, and a network of farmers to work with. We were happy, and if only ten people came a day, that was ten people we could share our story with.

There wasn't a menu, just a list of ingredients we were working with—fifty or so seasonal fruits, vegetables, plants, fish and meats from small suppliers, gardeners and growers, and what we could find in the wild. Every day we would produce somewhere between eighteen to twenty-five dishes, and there were always another twenty or so more in various stages of completion.

We had produced a pantry of dried wild leaves and flowers, cured meats, dried fish, oils, vinegars, pickles and ferments that were always on hand to help push us forward and keep us creative.

Our guests simply had to answer questions about dietary restrictions, tell us whether or not they wanted matching wines and decide on their number of courses—four, seven or nine. From there we would go about creating a menu especially for them based on the produce we had available on that particular day. Every dish served to our guests was a surprise. For them and for us. It was a conversation, an intimate exchange between strangers. We asked for their trust and in return we would create an experience just for them.

It was up to us to go above and beyond their expectations, to make them feel as though the trust they had given us had been rewarded.

Day in and day out it was a huge task. New dishes, new ingredients, new guests and repeat guests who came to expect completely new courses. We always had to create, always had to deliver. Push, push, push and keep pushing. I would tell myself over and over, 'We don't fail. We can do better.'

More often than not the day would start at about 6 am when, with blurry eyes, I would set off picking various plants along the train tracks. Or I would set the alarm for low tide to gather fresh sea lettuce and seawater for making cheese or brining, my head swimming with ideas of new dishes and flavours for the day's menu.

The day would wind up somewhere between 1 or 2 am because the workload demanded it. No one complained; with tired eyes and fatigued bodies we just got on with it. Before the reviews, before the media storm, we had all the time in the world—we just didn't know it yet.

it hits

Six months in and we had our first review, from Larissa Dubecki in *The Age*'s food liftout, Epicure. I remember the service being horrible—we were so behind I was butchering raw suckling pig to roast to order as we just hadn't had time to break it down that morning. We were flying blind, as we often did then, not knowing what was needed. Despite all that, the piece was titled 'When the food speaks for itself'. We got a 16/20 and were labelled 'a confident newcomer'. I was over the moon.

The day after that, the phone wouldn't stop ringing, with front of house having to work full-time just to take reservations. By the end of the day we were booked solid, but that was just the beginning. Later that week I heard Drew, one of our waiters, reading from *The Weekend Australian*—'Salt of the earth', the review by food writer and critic John Lethlean. It was the second major review in one week and it couldn't have been better for us. I mean, it can always be better, but we received four out of five 'Australians' and some very kind words, including the summary that we were 'raising the bar for regional Victoria'.

I was thrilled that we were being written about in such a positive way, it was so unexpected. But it was also a great opportunity to let go of our boundaries, to unleash all the little things I'd been too nervous to try and see where it would take us. In the following years Loam would go on to win numerous state and national awards including Regional Restaurant of the Year 2012 for *Gourmet Traveller*, along with a ranking of nineteenth best restaurant in Australia. We were awarded two hats, Best New Regional Restaurant and Dish of the Year for our 'suckling pig, cantaloupe and goat's curd' in *The Age Good Food Guide*. I was nominated for Chef of the Year, and named one of the '100 most influential people in Melbourne'. We had been featured in every magazine we could imagine. We were on cloud nine and our little restaurant was now on the national stage.

Booking requests intensified and our dining room was full every service. We were turning away more people than we could seat, and every service was thirty-five guests doing an average of seven courses. That was 245 plates of food per service, plus snacks and petits fours, all varying to some degree to meet the diners' expectations or dietaries. The pressure was on and all we had to cook with was a broken oven, a six-top stove with four working burners, two chefs, an eighteen-hour work day, sleep deprivation, and the constant drive to be better.

I should have seen it coming. Something was always going to break.

Today. Fucking today. Today is the day I get to find out my marriage is over. I discovered it in a message, a goddamn text message clearly not intended for me. What could be worse, you ask? Christ—I can't even scribble this down I'm shaking so badly—it's with a staff member, and that staff member is the only other chef I have. I don't believe it, but there it is right in front of me. I'm blindsided. Angry, hurt and betrayed. The rug's been pulled out from under me along with my restaurant, my career, my home, my partner, my staff. In one fucking text message my whole life has imploded. I feel like I've just had my throat cut, been left to bleed out on the floor and, as my breath weakens, they're plotting where to hide my body. This can't be happening. Can it?

just close the fucking thing

Loam was closed for eight weeks over the period it took for me to find
my feet and gather enough strength to open the doors and finish out
the last five months we had on the lease. These were the months it
would take to wind down the restaurant and execute a financial exit
plan, and they left me emotionally and physically exhausted. During
these months of working in an environment that had caused me so
much pain I simply fell out of love with cooking. In fact, I began to
loathe it. I began to really fucking hate it.

The produce I had once coveted so much—the tomatoes from
farmer Bruce Robinson I'd previously nurtured from farm to table, all
the things I had spent years raising—suddenly I didn't care if they were
left to rot in the dry store. The wild plants I'd picked carefully during
quiet mornings alone I now let wilt and die in the corner of the cool
room. All the charcuterie I had spent the previous year making I gave
away to anyone I could hand it to. I just couldn't stand looking at it.

I had fallen out of love with food, with cooking, with Loam and the
land around it. I was ready to give up. All the things that had given me
so much joy and pleasure for years were now things I wanted so badly
to remove from my life. I couldn't stomach any of them anymore. In my
eyes, cooking was the reason all this was happening. I had just lost my
best friend and wife, the business would soon be closed and I would
be out of a job. I would have to sell my home. In one fell swoop I had
lost it all—cooking had given me everything, and just as quickly taken
it all away.

And yet every day I had to stand in that kitchen, the place where
all this had happened. As far as I could see, cooking—food, the
restaurant—had caused this to happen. It had stripped me bare and
left me exposed and alone. I hated it all so much that I simply stopped
existing. I stopped eating; I was rapidly losing weight from an already
lanky frame. I became a ghost in a world that I had created and once
loved so much, I began to drink and sleep too much to mask the pain
of having to exist within it. I knew people were suspicious of why the
restaurant had closed for those eight weeks and it kept me awake
most nights. I could feel it from guests' covert looks and questions
left unasked but hanging in the air anyway. I retreated into myself,
pretended I had nothing to hide, smiled as if nothing had happened,
and answered their questions with dead tones and scripted lines.

It's a cold morning and there's a blue eye cod on the bench, just kinda lying there looking at me. I'm a thousand miles away inside my own head; the cod is bright-eyed and still in rigor, scales bright and sharp. I feel guilty because I just can't be bothered doing anything with it. I feel guilty the cod has ended up in this kitchen with me.

I wrestle with the idea of just throwing it in the bin and pretending it was never here, a thought that would have never crossed my mind before all of this. Or, maybe it would have—I can't remember much about who I was before all of this.

I decide to smoke the fish whole: a method that I don't really need to pay attention to, one that I can start and then leave to its own devices. I wipe it down, light a fire in the bottom of the smoker and hang it up to let the proteins slowly set. I don't need to think too much about it, I just need it done, somehow. There is no romance to this process. I have chosen it simply because it seems like the easiest way.

the last service

On the 28th of June, 2013, Loam closed, a day earlier than originally planned, and that evening I found myself standing in the cold, damp air of a Victorian winter, staring blankly into the shadows of the olive grove, depleted of all energy. Exhausted from a ninety-hour week and drinking far too much (to quiet all the emotional bullshit I was going through—well, that was what I was telling myself), I barely noticed that it had started to rain. Tired and numb, I didn't feel human anymore; emptied out to zero.

The restaurant behind me was still full of the last guests we ever served—friends and regulars, growers and suppliers, the people with whom over the few short years of our existence we had shared birthdays, anniversaries and milestones. They sounded happy and carefree, full of drunken excitement as they shared stories of their own past experiences at Loam. It's a world I truly wished I could be a part of that night, but I couldn't. I just couldn't face it and it made me so sad.

At that point I found myself starting to cry and I couldn't stop. I told myself I'd had enough, that I was letting go and that the end had finally arrived. That the restaurant was over and that now was the time to disappear.

Four weeks later and I would do exactly that. I would leave for America, flick the switch and self-destruct. Fuck cooking—fuck everything.

wood-smoked blue eye with soured cream and wild mustard

1 x 600 g (1 lb 5 oz) firm medium-sized blue eye cod
5 litres (170 fl oz/20 cups) fresh seawater
2 king edward potatoes, cut into 2 cm (¾ in) cubes
25 g (1 oz) dried kelp
15 wild mustard flowers, washed and dried

soured cream

250 ml (8½ fl oz/1 cup) jersey cream
½ teaspoon souring culture (BFlora – Type A)

serves 6–8 with left-over smoked fish

For the soured cream, warm the cream in a heavy-based saucepan until it reaches 36°C (97°F) or blood temperature (you can easily recognise this by sticking your finger in the cream—if it's the right temperature you won't feel a temperature difference). Remove from the heat and pour into a bowl, stir through the souring culture, cover with plastic wrap and leave to sit in a warm place overnight.

The next day, submerge the blue eye in a bucket filled with the seawater and leave to sit at room temperature for 1 hour. Remove from the water, dry thoroughly and set aside on a large tray.

Place a log of olive wood over a low flame and leave it to catch and start a small fire. Place the tray of cod near the fire but not so close that it will cook the fish too quickly; you want the protein to set slowly and take on as much smoke flavour as possible (alternatively, and better still, try hanging the blue eye a decent distance away from the flame). Leave the fish to smoke until the flesh feels like soft tofu and has started to turn from opaque to white. Remove from the heat, cover and leave to sit for 1 hour.

Wash the potato pieces in a bowl of cold water until soapy bubbles appear on the surface (that's the starch coming out). Transfer the potatoes and water to a large saucepan, bring to a simmer and cook for 6 minutes, until the potato pieces are tender but still retain a slight bite. Cover and transfer to the fridge to cool.

Put the kelp in a spice grinder and blitz to a fine powder.

Plate, including the mustard flowers, as you wish (there is no right way, and we often change it depending on the day and how everything falls on the plate). Use your intuition.

nashville

Nashville, the City of Lost and Broken Souls. That's what I called it anyway. Most call it Music City. Either way, no one I met during my time in this town was really from here. Instead it was a place people had just escaped to, gathered together and created something new. Some were in need of respite, others running from past lives, some still chasing youthful dreams—singers, songwriters, artists, people all in various states of repair or disrepair. It's exactly where I needed to be after Loam, foreign and alone, far away from cooking and anything familiar. The perfect place to lose myself, to not be me for a little while and to forget the shitstorm my life had turned into. A place where I could disappear from myself and everyone else.

A friend had offered me a couch to sleep on, that's how I ended up here. I'd gone from owning a successful restaurant and a house on the beach to sleeping on an undersized two-seat couch with a t-shirt for a pillow, everything I owned packed into a travel pack, a life condensed. I couldn't help looking down at my belongings, wondering how this had happened and where the fuck it had all gone wrong.

I wasn't really sleeping much either, aside from an hour or so here and there, but nothing that ever put my mind to rest. To fill the hours, I walked every day. Another form of escape—mainly from myself—doing something and nothing at the same time. I covered most of Nashville on foot, walking and thinking, crossing back and forth over the Cumberland River in the oppressive heat until it was finally time for happy hour at Puckett's, where I would drink pints of beer for $2 and eat BBQ chicken wings for less than 20 cents each until I passed out, then wake up and do it all again.

It's funny; I used to be a successful chef—right? Just a month earlier I had been listed in the Swedish magazine *Fool* as one of the 100 most underrated chefs in the world. Now I was on my own in a foreign city for the first time in I can't remember how long. I had nowhere to be, no obligations, nothing. It was such an odd feeling compared to the non-stop work and eighteen-hour days of the last eight years.

I couldn't ever remember being that idle, being alone with no responsibility and no accountability. It didn't really suit me, I was slowly beginning to realise. I needed something to focus on, something to obsess over, something to wake me the fuck up!

nashville hot chicken

I still remember my first bite of Nashville hot chicken. I remember where I was sitting (third table on the left), I remember the music—a scratchy country song lamenting the plight of the South—and I remember the smell, ah the smell, a mixture of sweet paprika and fiery chilli. It's a picture that is burnt into my memory.

I was wearing a white t-shirt, which turned out to be a rookie mistake. It's hot out, about 90 degrees with 85 per cent humidity, and we were all dripping with sweat just from walking through the parking lot. I was with Brian, a chef who had just moved to Nashville from L.A., and my friend Trisha, who was in town visiting from Australia. We had set off across town to try this chicken we'd all heard about but not yet tasted.

I ordered the dark meat, hot, with blue cheese sauce and fries. I remember it exactly. The crunch, the sweetness, the smell of spices and the heat, that addictive heat… What the fuck had just happened to me? Something as simple as fried chicken had roused something in me I hadn't felt since what seemed like a lifetime ago, at Loam. It was a sense of surprise, excitement, curiosity. Something so simple but so disarming. It was the feeling that I needed to figure it out; I needed to work out how to cook it. For the first time in a very long time I found myself at the edge of something I couldn't understand but actually wanted to.

From there that chicken became a sort of obsession or addiction. I had to have it. And if I wasn't already thinking about it, all it would take was a mention and I'd need a fix.

It was better than drugs, I guess.

existing

It didn't take me long to make plans to eat at every hot chicken restaurant in Nashville. In fact, fried chicken pretty much became my entire diet. Shockingly, I talked to friends who had lived there for years who had never had it. It made me wonder if I should know them at all.

I'd started to work in town. I needed the money—I'd been burning through most of my savings just existing in limbo and, having rented an apartment downtown, I had to figure out how to pay for it. It was a small kitchen with a small crew not at all interested in the industry or even doing a good job—paycheque kids with somewhere better to be. The menu was simple, perhaps a little too simple. Shared plates, very Melbourne, and in that sense a concept pretty foreign for Nashville.

The owner was an over-the-top, seemingly lovely Southern lady who greeted everyone with a 'Hey y'all' and 'Well, ain't that peachy' attitude. Southern charm, they told me, before adding the ominous warning that you also charm snakes. I wasn't really sure what she wanted from me, but I knew that she needed some help; the menu was terrible, the staff questionable, the drinks good, the place failing. Nothing about the job made me want to cook and I knew the place couldn't be saved but it was money, plus something I could do, for now, something to replace the fatigue of living in purgatory existing to exist, walking and walking, waiting for something, anything.

And it meant I could go and eat that chicken. The plan was to start with Prince's, out on Nolensville Pike, the originators and spiritual home of hot chicken, and end up at the new kids on the block, Hattie B's, over near Vanderbilt. In between we'd hit Pepperfire, representing East Nashville, and Bolton's, an old school shack on Gallatin Pike. All different restaurants honouring the tradition and recipes of Nashville hot chicken. Each interpreting this delicacy in their own way. I wanted to taste them all.

I can't believe I'm about to board this plane. About to drink my last Miller High Life and eat my last bologna sandwich, to say goodbye to the few thrift shop belongings I've accumulated this year and placed as talismans in my light-filled apartment that looks out over downtown, and from where, with the windows open, the shouts and shrieks of drunks have kept me company all through the night. I've grown to like Nashville and the way nothing seems real here—the façade the city throws up seems to help bury the everyday reality of life. Nashville feels like home to me because I don't feel real myself, so why am I about to board this plane?

Whatever the reason, I've decided to go back, but I'm stronger now, I think. I know I have unfinished business at home, and I want my career back. I thought I could work for someone else, cooking food I don't care about for people who don't care either, but it turns out I was wrong. There is a voice telling me not to do it, but there's another, stronger, louder voice telling me I have to.

The problem I've found here isn't my inability to escape and become invisible, it's that no matter how hard I try to outrun my demons they always follow. No matter where I go, or which shadowy bar I try and drown them in, they always reappear.

I argue with myself the whole time, debating whether to actually get on the plane—thinking about the cons of going home, not the pros of hopefully starting a new restaurant, which don't come into play. I board anyway—I've paid for the ticket—order a gin, and double drop Temazepam (a pre-flight ritual that helps curb the hostilities of a long-haul flight) before falling into ten hours of sleep.

above: Port Phillip Bay cuttlefish

PART 1 2016

JO VIGNI

january

'I'm trying to get better
because I haven't been
my best.'
Frank Turner

I'm sitting on a box, alone in the dining room that in a few weeks will come alive, that will live and breathe for the first time as IGNI, quietly reflecting on the last few years. How on earth have I got to this point? I feel like I've lived a hundred different lives in the past two years, and I'm wondering if my love of cooking will return, because right now, sitting in a half-built restaurant, I don't feel like it will.

> I still wonder how I ended up here, with a restaurant in a laneway in the centre of Geelong. I wonder if I've made the right decision. 'Well, at least it was a decision,' I catch myself saying under my breath. They're something I've avoided making with any consistency for the last two years.

It's strangely quiet here, until a middle-aged couple pop their heads through the open door and ask if this is the new restaurant by Aaron Turner. 'We heard it was down here—we have been walking the streets trying to find it,' they tell me. I reply cheekily that 'It is, but he's not here right now.' They ask to make a booking so they won't miss out like they did the three times they tried to book at Loam. I take down their details, smile politely and send them happily on their way.

I feel a thousand years away from the person I used to be, disconnected from everything. I feel so different sitting here alone thinking of the months to come, the inevitable ghosts of past lives that will rear their heads.

The restaurant itself doesn't even feel real yet, despite the fact that I'm sitting in it. I've had a hard time watching it being built, between the impending sense of dread, and wondering if I can make it work or at least hold up my end of the bargain, and the delays have come as somewhat of an expensive reprieve.

It's now or never, I tell myself, and close my eyes.

14·01·2016
(6 days to opening)

I'm so frustrated right now, trying to pick up where I left off two-and-a-half years ago when I stopped cooking, dropped it all and walked away, and today in this new kitchen the idea of cooking again, trying to cook again, it just isn't working. It's shit; I'm shit; I can feel the frustration and anxiety building up, the panic and self-doubt, the constant questioning of myself, my skills, my talent, and whether or not any of it even exists anymore and thinking it probably doesn't, a cloud that won't seem to lift.

If I'm honest, I'm scared—terrified—and questioning whether or not this was a good idea.

top: Rowan Andrews, Jono Hall, Jo Smith
below: Drew Hamilton, Aaron Turner

Nothing makes sense, and nothing's working.

All the places that had once inspired me, the places I'd go to pick wild grasses, herbs, seaweed from the beaches, plants from the inlets, roadsides and farms, the places I understood, the places that were a big part of the reason I returned to this area to cook, no longer make sense. None of these places fill me with joy anymore. I feel even more disconnected from everything I know and have ever felt about cooking, and about time and place. Maybe that's it—perhaps this place has passed me by. Perhaps it's too late for me.

> I've tried and failed at re-starting all the pickles and ferments I would have in the pantry at Loam, staples that I used to rely on to have around when I needed them. Simple preparations that if treated right at the beginning could take care of themselves, no real attention needed. Things I've successfully made hundreds of times before but not here, not in this new environment and not with a fire burning all day. Turns out that this room, with the exhaust fan turned off overnight and the embers slowly dying, is too hot, and that, coupled with the summer's heat, has managed to cook or stew most of the pickles I've been working on. Jesus Christ, really? I can't even get that right.

There is nothing about this new restaurant that is exciting me yet. Actually, it's the exact opposite, and the more I try and fail the more I can't think, eat, taste or see beyond these walls.

I'm trying desperately to figure all this out, but all I seem to know is that right now I hate this, I hate cooking. It's failing me, or I'm failing it.

There's nothing much to write about or say, today, it was just more of the same shit and failures. It's not hard to make an anglaise, but I've managed to scramble the eggs three times before giving up. The fire is frustrating me, the heat, the imperfection of it all.

I have to figure something out soon. We have a restaurant to open, we need to be ready, we need a plan, and I know most of this hinges on me leading the way, showing what we are doing in the kitchen, but I'm stumbling around at the moment trying to figure it all out in my own head. I wish we had more time, but I'm not sure it would make much of a difference.

All this with what feels like thousands of eyes on me; even if they aren't, it feels like it.

I am drowning under the weight of my own expectations.

Why did I choose to cook over fire and only fire? At least I can blame that, if this doesn't work.

If I can't get it right, I can take solace in the fact that I didn't know how to use it, the fire—will that be enough?

I decide to light the fire a little earlier than we have been, just to have it burning in the background, and perhaps even give us a little inspiration.

I don't fully understand it yet. I've never worked with direct flame before, not like this, not as the only source of cooking in a commercial kitchen, using it to service a dining room full of guests. It's the centrepiece of the kitchen, the life of it all. It has changed the way I interact with cooking. Every day is different because the fire behaves according to its own will. It has a life of its own, a certain energy and curiosity that demands constant attention. The trade-off is the calmness at the centre of it, and the realisation that we are never really in control.

> And it's then, in a bizarre moment of, let's call it clarity, it hits me: the fire behaves the way I've always cooked, the way I see produce—always different and always changing with the days, and the months, and the weather, even the fuel used to feed it.

This is the same as the way a duck in winter will taste different to a duck in spring, the same way a pear in early autumn will only suggest what a pear will taste like later in the same month, so why treat it the same way, when they are really two different things? The perfect dish week in and week out is so unappealing to me. I don't chase any regimented consistency; as a cook I try to avoid it at all costs, choosing instead to let the produce guide me. It's a kind of freedom most kitchens or cooks don't have—instead they are often resigned to producing the same dishes for months on end.

Now the fire is offering me that same freedom from consistency, the freedom to know that it is different every day, and, therefore, so the food should be.

That realisation aside, I still have no idea what dishes we will open with. I know we need at least sixteen to start, but I have no idea what they are or even what they could possibly be. What I do have is a better knowledge of the fire, and tomorrow I will wipe away all the plans I have made up to this point. The new potatoes barely the size of a fingernail that I have previously subjected to sous vide, vacuum packed in olive oil and placed in a water bath in a dark corner of the kitchen and forgotten for 20 minutes instead will be coated in clarified butter and slowly roasted over the fire high on the grill and above any direct heat, which allows them to roast slowly, the outside of the tiny potatoes crisping while the insides steam to a creamy earthiness. The flavour is amazing: these little bursts taste more like potato than I can remember. There is something so comforting in the flavour that it brings a wide smile. It's a brief moment where I remember the joys of cooking. It's been a while.

With this realisation all the prep I've intended or attempted to start I will scrap, a thousand lines and scribbles in my notebook all crossed out. I will start again, simpler, smarter this time. Tomorrow with new excitement I'll begin at the very beginning and start working on snacks.

above: Merryn Campbell

Ok, if I don't start cooking now and giving the front of house something to taste, not only will we not have any food but we won't have any wines matched to sell the package we want to offer.

We have always been good at matching wines to our food, searching for obscure varietals to work new, unique angles of the ingredients, rather than safe and obvious, straight up-and-down assumed home runs. It's fun to play with the unexpected and get people drinking something they normally wouldn't.

I've started with the Point Henry saltbush; it grows everywhere here and is something I've used for years. I've wrapped cheese with it, pickled it, made a terrible-tasting ice cream with it, grilled and sautéed it, but it's my love of salt and vinegar chips that led me to flash fry it to bring out the natural salt and then dust it with powdered vinegar. Nature's healthy alternative to salt and vinegar chips and the perfect snack to start with a pre-dinner drink. I'd previously served this at Loam, just before the end, and I didn't want to repeat anything, but I guess it's inevitable, I tell myself, and allow this one inclusion.

I put it on the pass for everyone to taste, and as I start to explain it to the front of house I see a comforting smile from Jo and Drew. I take a deep breath. First snack done.

salt and vinegar saltbush

I still have a long way to go, especially since the ideas and notes that survived for the first dishes still aren't really working. I've scrapped almost all of them, persisting with the few ideas I'm convinced will work and that I still like the sound of.

I'm trying to convince myself that a coconut ice cream and parsley sauce would be the perfect dessert to start with, but I'm rushing it and can't quite get it to work. In some sort of strange moment—why, I'm not sure—I think that maybe cherries will tie it all together.

But they don't and the dessert is bad, horrible in fact. I decide to ditch it and go back to it when I have more time. Or maybe it's just a shit idea, never to be returned to. I'll leave it for now—I've lost a lot of valuable hours to it already.

The ducks and squabs are hanging and have been ageing for two weeks, and we've stuffed them with dried wild grasses and hay to help dry them out and impart a sweet, earthy flavour. They are taking care of themselves, prep-wise, but I've yet to figure out what to do with them.

Bruce is back on the team and he is picking and harvesting for me this morning, so I'll wait and see what he comes back with, hoping for some inspiration.

We open in two days and are still nowhere close to being ready. The more the pressure builds the more I'm not sure I will get it done and the more real the fear of failure becomes.

above: hay-smoked duck (page 80)

19·01·2016
(day before opening)

I threw up this morning, in the shower, just as I always do before opening. If I'm honest, it's every morning for the first few weeks. We have a long way to go yet, and my body knows it. Still, it's nice to see Jo and Drew excited about it all, even if I'm not full of confidence that we'll be ok. I can see through Jo's façade that she's stressed about it all, but they have done an amazing job turning this space into our new home.

1 pm

There have been some minor victories this morning: the grilled lettuce dish seems to be working—the cos heart, brined for twenty minutes, brushed with olive oil and grilled over a high heat right above the ironbark embers quickly crisps the outer leaves while softening the core and creates a nice balance of charred, sweet young leaves and soft bitterness. I've always liked the flavour of cooked lettuce, and I'm surprised just how much heat the leaves can take. The whole process of brining and grilling the leaves is reminiscent of meat and how we treat it before cooking—something I'd like to think more about when I have the mental space again.

4·30 pm

Bruce arrives with bags, boxes and trays of fruits and vegetables, leaves and various other questionable, and in his words, perhaps edible, things.

Among it all I see what looks like purslane, but it's not like the wild stuff I used to pick from the side of the road, it's in flower and looks exactly like a rose just before it unfurls. Bruce calls it rainbow purslane, followed by a story of receiving an unnamed packet of seeds in the mail. He can't quite recall ordering them but he's mildly convinced that perhaps it was after a long afternoon in the garden and a bottle or two of cheap red.

> I immediately start to chew, and it's crazy. Imagine a savoury lemon, one you could eat like an apple, the stalk as crisp as celery. It is sour and bitter yet strangely piquant. Bruce tells me he's growing it behind the makeshift greenhouse in his special blend of soil (which I don't ask about). He assures me as much as he can that it won't kill me, and will therefore make me stronger.

Straight away I start thinking about this with the squab. Perhaps I'll make a sauce with it, blend it with some anchovies, parsley, a little lemon for more acid and use that... Then it hits me—the purslane already has all that I want it to have. It's a balanced taste without me doing a thing to it, so why manipulate it if I don't need to? Why fuck with it, why not just serve the squab with the fresh purslane? A plant perfectly in season, everything we as cooks should strive for.

I check with Bruce to see if we will have access to it fresh every day. Then I remember the bag of wild plums Mum picked for me the previous day. I'll make a quick sauce of reduced plum juice with a little anise and clove and slice cheeks fresh for every plate. Simple.

I'll have three things on a plate at peak ripeness, no manipulation, and the most important thing is that we can concentrate on cooking the squab perfectly over the fire, instead of dividing our attention working on five separate elements needed for one dish. And so another dish is settled.

aged squab/wild plum/rainbow purslane

above: Bruce Robinson

I'm standing at the pass in my shiny new kitchen, staring at the white plates that I hate. Every table is set with them and they stare up at me, mocking me. I hate these plates; they are so generic, so impersonal, bleached and cast within an inch of their lives. The ones we wanted were beautiful—Australian made, hand dyed—but we couldn't afford them because we ran out of money, spent it all on silicone, hooks, curtain rods, storage shelves, and a thousand other things no one will ever even see. So here we are with two-dollar generic white plates, harmless enough but Jesus Christ. In the weeks and months of madness we had forgotten about them, the need for them, and now on the morning of opening we have foot soldiers scouring the city for something, anything decent, something in any way usable. I hate that we forgot such a detail.

> No guests have arrived yet, but soon they will; the restaurant is quiet, like it's holding its breath. It's eerie, waiting in near silence for the first guests to walk through the door and shatter this fragile sense of calm. In thirty minutes they will sit and judge every aspect of our hard work over the last year. They will scan the finish of the floor, question the choice of colour, discuss the decision-making behind our serviceware, uniforms, lights. Then they will move on to judging the food. I feel nauseous, almost transparent.

I crack my knuckles and press my fists into my lower back, arching to relieve the stiffness. I hear the kitchen behind me, fresh with excitement and courage—the young chefs we really can't afford are eager and ready to go. I can't share their innocent excitement this time around.

I hang my head, the weight of expectation growing, my chest tightening, my breathing heavy.

Are we ready?

Does it even matter?

7·05 pm   The first service is here and we are sinking. I can see the confusion on the floor. The kitchen is sedate but functioning, kind of, just waiting for the storm. We have reached the point of hoping to just get through it, survive tonight, hold our heads up high as people leave, and then lick our wounds and console ourselves with stiff drinks to find the resolve to right the ship as best we can tomorrow.

Did I really expect to just pick up as normal after more than two years had passed, and think everything would work? It's insane.

7·35 pm   The dining room is filling with smoke. Yup, filling with smoke from the fire we are cooking on. It's the specialized extraction system we paid a fortune for and built especially to extract live fire—it doesn't seem to be extracting anything. In fact, it's doing the exact opposite. It worked fine all week, but still, I shouldn't be surprised that on opening night it breaks. Of course it would, why wouldn't it? Why would a brand new $16,000+ extraction unit work?

We push on despite watery eyes and smoke-filled lungs. The guests don't seem to mind, the brave-faced front-of-house team have reassured them that it's all part of the show; however, I can see that they are deeply concerned that we are about to catch fire.

I can't help but think again, Why have I done this? Why have I put myself through all of this, just to fuck it all up?

I was happy in Nashville, I think. I was restless, sure, but I'm always restless, it's my nature. I've never been able to sit still, so everyone tells me.

So what's worse, idle and restless, or drowning in a sea of your own making?

8 pm

I'm not happy with the food, not at all, but then again was I ever really happy with it? Everything looks and tastes just a little insipid, mainly because we are scared of the fire and not using it the best we can. It's frustrating because I know it's the lack of understanding. We pieced together the menu from new realisations, thoughts and processes, ones we barely understood, and they all came a little too late for us to define or refine the dishes we are cooking tonight.

I'm so disappointed with myself today, and I feel embarrassed standing here pretending to be a cook, exposed to a room full of people, wide open for all to see. What makes it worse is that tonight— on opening night—every guest has chosen to do eight courses with a wine pairing.

It's a disaster. The worst-case scenario for our first service. In hindsight I can't understand why we didn't see it coming—a room full of friends and family, of course they would all order the maximum amount of food and wine. They all had good intentions and were excited to be there. The truth is we simply weren't ready.

240 plates of food + snacks
240 glasses of wine + pre-dinner drinks
3 front of house
3 chefs
1 fire

It's a suicide mission.

9 pm

The first of the guests are starting to leave. I can see them paying and making small talk with Drew and Jo. It's one of the few tables we don't know, just regular excited guests who have come to see what we are doing. An intense rush of panic comes over me. What if they want to talk to me? To tell me how bad their evening was, just how disappointed they are and that they now will have to get everything dry cleaned because of the smoke. There's nowhere to hide, nowhere to take cover from the inevitable conversation.

Luckily they have no interest in talking to me and head home, leaving me to try and focus on the next few hours and the long road towards ending our first service.

opposite: aged lamb rump/raw honey
vinegar/radicchio and parsnip (page 120)

1 am

Everyone has gone home and I'm alone in the kitchen making peace with the first night of service. I must have wiped the same three benches twenty-five times thinking about those fucking white plates; they won't stop tormenting me. After 17 hours and 240 courses, they're the only solid thing I can wrap my mind around.

I need to sleep. I haven't really slept at all recently, a million different thoughts racing through my mind, all fighting for head space and often colliding into one another. Though together they add up to nothing at all, they are, nonetheless, keeping me wide awake in a suspended sense of dread and panic that this isn't going well.

It takes several cups of black coffee before I can talk myself into going back to work. I'm a little weary and battle-worn from last night. It's been a long time since I've had to do a service that required absolute concentration, but I will put on a brave face and resolve to survive another day.

There's a sense of team spirit, a feeling of let's make it better, let's kick some ass even if we don't know how yet. There are a few adjustments to some of the dishes that I want to make: I need to chiffonade the fermented cabbage for the hanger steak and, while I'm thinking of it, reduce the portion size as well—it's too much protein after seven courses, but perhaps the right amount for five.

The sauce for the dish needs a little work too, it's a little off balance. We are using the vinegar from pickled leek flowers to finish it off. I'll taste it again, but I think some freshly cracked pepper might bring it into line.

We need to work on plating also, it got very scrappy in the heat of last night's service. I don't really like any of our plates, they're all far too glossy. We ordered them off a Swedish website that made them look better than the reality: white, simple, classic, but really they are cheaply finished everyday plates.

We have nineteen people booked in tonight; fingers crossed we can do a better job.

I've spent a lot of time today considering if I have anything to give anymore, moments of complete emptiness at a time I should feel energised and excited about the future and this new adventure. It's a strange feeling, one I'm trying to make sense of.

We had some squid delivered this morning—one of my favourite things to eat—I'm not sure what to do with it but it was just too good to pass up, the reflective fluorescent greens still glistening. I'll show Rowan how to clean it and perhaps we can slice it paper thin, raw, but for now I'll just get it prepped so it's not wasted.

It's quieter tonight, twelve booked. It's funny how the task of feeding twelve people can take its toll; I'm tired from the week already, and there are still three more services to go.

Luke and Deb are eating tonight. Luke and I came up together in the cooking world, opened our first restaurants at the same time, connected in the way only cooks can, for the love of what we do, an understanding, a bond that's so uniquely shared between cooks all over the world. Deb is his partner and also a chef. They have flown in from Sydney to cook a special lunch tomorrow. We arranged the date months earlier, before we opened, when we were on track to have been open for months already by this time.

I find myself apologising to them between courses; I'm nervous and I feel bad that they are experiencing IGNI this way, unprepared and bumbling around like an awkward teenager. I know Luke's palate and I know he'll see the mistakes. I can't hide them.

It's a conversation over the squab, a leg aged on the carcass for fourteen days, started cold on the grill and roasted far away from any direct flame but catching a flare every so often as the rendering fat hits the charcoal. The texture sparks Luke's curiosity; it's chewy in a gelatinous way, much like the knuckle of a pig trotter. Luke asks if I had confit them before they hit the grill. I hadn't. In fact it never even occurred to me, I just left them on top of the grill to cook slowly, it just made sense.

And it's then, a light-bulb fuck-me moment—*just cook*. Stop thinking and just cook.

It's been an exhausting first week. Luke's Sunday lunch wasn't planned to happen in our first week, but here he is, and here we are about to prep a new menu, with a new chef in a new kitchen, four days after we opened. It's madness. Luke cooks a lot like me—needing to see, touch, taste and smell the produce and ingredients before knowing what to do with them. Among the madness of the first week and a few brief text messages at the end of each service I've ordered a couple of extra squabs and saved enough of the duck from Great Ocean Ducks that I have ageing in the cool room, these birds lovingly raised and fed on the season's fruits and vegetables, happy ducks free to roam, peck, swim and waddle. I have never seen or cooked duck quite as good as this before, it's truly one of the best products here in Australia, and right on our doorstep.

I've managed to get a hold of a few kilos of fresh king george whiting hours out of the bay and twenty minutes from IGNI. I have organised Bruce, as best I can, to pick the best of the morning's herbs and leaves. He has promised me white mulberries, so long as he remembers to set his alarm to beat the birds.

Luke is bringing with him sake lees that a mutual friend of ours has brought back from Japan. There is talk of making an ice cream with them but everything else we will work out this morning, creating a menu based on what we have right here in front of us, a reaction to the day and produce, a menu made in a moment and then gone. This is real cooking, to me there is no other way—it's the only way I know how, now that I've finally remembered.

I'm excited to have Luke here, it's like therapy. Today it feels like all the pressure is off me and I can try to enjoy just being here in the kitchen.

What a great lunch we had with Luke and Deb. It was nice to cook with old friends again, and I think it was also nice for them to have free rein in a brand new kitchen. Creating the menu first thing in the morning and cooking for the love of it, building a fire, telling old stories—the kitchen has become like a campfire, comforting.

> We sit and share Sunday night family meal together with the staff, and for the first time I convince myself to relax and enjoy the company I'm in. For the first time I can sit in relative calmness, in a space that is now alive and breathing, and beginning ever so slowly to find its own identity.

It's a quiet day today, prepping and cleaning, getting ready for our first full week of service.

We only have twelve reservations, which comes as somewhat of a relief.

I'm concerned that many of the dishes aren't balanced, some things are slightly off, hurried, or perhaps not fully formed. I'm used to that feeling, somewhat, it's how I cook, but something more is bugging me about it. Maybe it's a reflection of my current head space, or perhaps it's a lactic thing? That's always played a big role in my cooking, using wheys and milks as a way of seasoning and finishing dishes. I have tried to avoid that here, wanting to be as far away from my old style as I could be in order to avoid the comparison with my cooking at Loam. But maybe I've gone too far from it. Or maybe I'm simply losing my touch.

Today is a slow day, and there's a sombre mood among the staff that matches the weather. It's our first full week as IGNI, five services. I hadn't noticed that it started to rain earlier, but it seems to be getting louder as the afternoon goes on, and it just keeps coming. I've seen it rain this hard before in the tropics, but not here, and not for this long.

'CHEEEEEEEEF, the office is flooding!' I hear Rowan, one of my chefs, say.

The roof above our tiny office/closet has burst open and water is pouring in all over the switchboard and computers. Everything that shouldn't get wet is getting poured on, soaked.

We band together to bail water out of the office as quickly as we can, using anything we can—saucepans, brooms, kitchen towels— getting everything we can to higher ground.

It's then we notice that the deluge is forcing its way through the front windows. It turns out that today is Geelong's storm of the century, and IGNI is flooding, fast.

All hands scramble to start sweeping out water, building makeshift barriers out of tea towels and attempting to mop away the water, but as fast as we can clear the rain it comes back in. I can't help thinking about sinking ship comparisons, but it feels like one of those moments where all you can do is laugh just to keep yourself from crying. Water is finding its way in through any small hole and the roof is now a waterfall. All we can do is sit and wait for the rain to stop, clean up, survey the damage and piece what we can of our restaurant back together. We decide there is too much that needs to be fixed, so in what was to be our first full week of business, we have to close for the night. We will have to call all of our reservations, some of whom have already started the trip down from Melbourne, and explain to them why we won't be opening. We will have to explain to them that our restaurant is now a swimming pool.

We are able to open up the next night, luckily for us, and the rest of the week unfolds with little other drama, apart from all the mistakes you make trying to find your feet as a new restaurant. That is until Sunday when our first reviewer walks through the doors. And it's a big one.

It's *Gourmet Traveller*, the national food magazine.

the first review

12·30 pm

It's that feeling in your stomach, that one where it feels like you're in freefall, when your plane suddenly drops altitude; it's a cross between nausea and adrenaline, excitement and absolute terror. That moment when you see for the first time someone walk though the doors who will write about you, and your restaurant, and their experience. A review that people all over the country will read, the first national exposure we will have as a new restaurant, a review in a credited national magazine or newspaper. They will look at the place you have nurtured and turned from a vacant building into a home, a functioning space made up of your best intentions, dreams, hope and fears, a place where it's you and no one else.

I let the kitchen know that NOTHING LEAVES THIS KITCHEN WITHOUT MY EYES and nothing gets sent without me tasting it and approving it, now everyone get your shit together and DO NOT FUCK THIS UP, but it's more of a warning to myself than to them.

5·30 pm

I couldn't even begin to tell how that went. I have no idea. It's a blur. Our first Sunday service and we have been reviewed. I analyse every aspect of the service that I can remember and still can't seem to grasp how it went. Drew is convinced the reviewer loved it, but that's Drew for you, the eternal optimist. I'm the eternal realist. We debate between us all the things that went right and wrong.

A cold sweat comes over me as I contemplate fucking it up, completely, for everyone. How was the seasoning? Was it all too simple? Did we manage to convince him we know what we are doing? Was the cooking ok? I know I wasn't happy with the butter, but did we do all that we could to show that we are a fully functioning restaurant ticking all the boxes that would make him write a positive review that will convince others that we do indeed know what we are doing?

Do we even know what we are doing? Thousands of doubts and thoughts race through my mind. I didn't even want to open this restaurant, did I? What compelled me to ever begin this journey, or even return to cooking?

I hated cooking. I hated it. I have no place doing this anymore.

Ahh fuck it, it's done now.

Drew and I console ourselves with 'We can always sell the space.'

Michael Harden   *Gourmet Traveller*   Published 1 2 . 0 2 . 2 0 1 6

Aaron Turner has made a triumphant return to the restaurant world and his cooking, at IGNI in Geelong, is better than ever.

The confidence is apparent almost immediately.

After negotiating the choice of five or eight courses (the number more guide than hard-and-fast rule), the meal begins with snacks. They're the same snacks for every table, the only time during the meal you could be eating exactly the same thing as your fellow diners. It's a wise move because missing any of these little flavour bombs would leave you feeling cheated.

Local saltbush leaves, fried crisp and then sprinkled with vinegar powder, are like hipster salt and vinegar chips, aesthetically pleasing and texturally interesting. Zucchini flowers are stuffed with pieces of pickled mussels and then grilled over charcoal. Squares of chicken skin are roasted to a cracker-like crunchiness and spread with a superb, citrusy cod-roe paste, while tiny ear-shaped slices of house-made guanciale and twig-like lengths of beef jerky (marinated in a mix of mushroom soy sauce, vinegar, grapeseed oil, and dried herb and fish paste before being dehydrated) round out the big flavours.

The name IGNI may not exactly roll off the tongue, but it's a good fit here with its nods to fire and ignition. Literally, it refers to the charcoal in the kitchen that features in so many of the restaurant's dishes. But with Aaron Turner cooking as well as this after years away and a series of life-changing events, it's hard to avoid the new-beginning, rising-from-the-ashes connotations.

Whichever way you want to take it, IGNI is a name you should remember and a restaurant you should eat at. Time to pay Geelong a visit.

salt and vinegar saltbush

This snack is a mainstay in the restaurant and with good reason—everyone loves chips. The vinegar powder we use here is the same freeze-dried white vinegar powder used on commercial salt and vinegar varieties.

grapeseed oil, for deep-frying
100 g (3½ oz) point henry saltbush leaves (about 3–4 saltbush branches, leaves stripped)
white vinegar powder, for sprinkling

makes 100 g (3½ oz)

Half-fill a saucepan with grapeseed oil and heat to 180°C (350°F), or until a leaf dropped into the oil is surrounded by rapidly forming tiny bubbles.

Add the leaves to the pan in 2–3 batches and fry until crisp. Remove from the hot oil and place on paper towel to drain, then sprinkle over the vinegar powder and serve.

seawater-cured scallop

6 scallops in their shells
1 litre (34 fl oz/4 cups) fresh seawater
20 g (¾ oz) wild scampi roe

serves 6 as a snack

Gently pry the scallop shells open using the back of a knife, sliding the blade underneath the scallop muscle to detach it from the shell. Rinse the scallop shells and set aside.

With a sharp knife, remove the stomach and gills from the scallop meat. Detach the roes and set aside for another use, then add the scallop meat to a bowl filled with the seawater and refrigerate overnight.

Remove the scallops from the seawater, lightly rinse in fresh water and dry between paper towels, then thinly slice and return to the shells. Cover with the scampi roe and serve.

roasted oysters/seawater emulsion/oyster leaf

I first came across the sea succulent oyster leaf when I was travelling and working in Spain, where it was on one of the dishes we served. I was so amazed by how similar its flavour was to an actual oyster that when I returned and opened Loam, I asked Bruce if he could get hold of any. After a lot of trawling he came across some on a Spanish website and ordered a hundred seeds. Only fifty turned up in the post (the others got lost) but those he did get his hands on he successfully grew and he now continues to cultivate them, hand-pollinating the plants every year. A unique and special plant.

12 large oysters
1 egg, plus 1 yolk
½ teaspoon dijon mustard
210 ml (7 fl oz) grapeseed oil
splash of rice vinegar
salt flakes
6 fresh oyster leaves

serves 6 as a snack

Bury the oysters in the embers of a slow fire and leave to cook for about 7 minutes, or until the tops start to pop open. Remove from the heat and chill.

Once cool, carefully shuck the oysters, removing any pieces of shell and reserving the brine.

Add the brine and half the oysters to a blender together with the egg, egg yolk and dijon mustard and blitz on a high speed for 1 minute. Scrape down the sides, then continue to blitz on a medium speed, gradually adding the grapeseed oil, until the mixture has thickened slightly. Add the rice vinegar and season with salt to taste.

To serve, spoon the blended oyster mixture back into six of the shells, top each with a whole oyster and serve with the oyster leaves.

aged squab/wild plum/rainbow purslane

The wild plums that I use for this sauce come from the side of the road on the way to Colac. I've been picking them for years, and whenever my parents come to visit during the season they bring me a few kilos, risking cuts and bruises from the wild trees. The plums have a really balanced flavour and at their freshest we serve them as is—fresh fruit to end the meal. Once they've gone past that stage is when we turn them into a sauce.

Be sure to use purslane that is in flower, has started to open and is still quite crisp when chewed—the flavour will be at its most fresh and alive at this point.

> 2 x 200 g (7 oz) squab (pigeon), washed and thoroughly dried
> clarified butter, for brushing
> 1 bunch flowering rainbow purslane

wild plum sauce

> 500 g (1 lb 2 oz) wild plums (blood plums will also work)
> 2 star anise
> 2 teaspoons coriander seeds
> 3 cloves
> 1 fresh bay leaf
> 3 tablespoons cider vinegar
> 2 tablespoons rock sugar
> 2 tablespoons caster (superfine) sugar
> splash of apple-cider vinegar

serves 4

Stuff the squab cavities and underneath the wings with dried grass or hay and leave to hang in a cool place for at least 14 days. Once aged, wipe the squab down with a damp cloth and remove the legs, head, wishbone and wings, setting aside the legs and reserving the rest for making a broth later.

For the wild plum sauce, add all the ingredients to a large heavy-based saucepan and cover with filtered water. Cover the pan with plastic wrap, bring to a simmer and leave to cook for 1 hour, then remove the plastic wrap, reduce the heat and cook for a further hour. Strain, pushing the mix gently through a fine sieve. Keep warm.

Roast the squab crown over a medium fruitwood fire until rare, brushing with clarified butter as it cooks, then leave to rest in a warm spot. Add the squab legs to the fire and roast slowly, moving them around the heat and brushing with clarified butter as you go, until crisp.

Plate, including the rainbow purslane, as you wish.

february

03·02·2016

I've decided to make some changes, to get rid of some of the dishes from last week that I don't like or that I feel are the weakest. It's an effort to streamline our learning.

We usually aim for anywhere between twelve and twenty-two different dishes for the menu and for the front of house to utilise when creating a tailored experience for our guests. We need to have a variety of dishes so that we can accommodate our guests' needs, wants and desires, but for tonight and for the remainder of the week, I'm stripping it down to only ten. This won't give us a lot of room to manoeuvre but I'll deal with dietaries and dislikes when and if they occur. This week I just want the kitchen to concentrate on ten dishes only and really nail them, hopefully building our confidence in the process.

For the most part I've managed to put Sunday's review out of my mind. I can't change it now. I wish I could, but I can't, and this week we really have to knuckle down and work out this path to being the restaurant we want to be.

07·02·2016

It feels like we have taken our foot off the pedal a little. I'm not sure why, maybe it's the shell shock of opening and being reviewed in the second week, maybe it's the realisation that we now have a restaurant that is open, with real guests paying real money. I've noticed a difference in service—the energy isn't there, it's more timid, nervous. It has very quickly become perfunctory, for what reasons I'm not sure.

> Our service and restaurant should be full of positive energy and personality, our guests feed off it, that certain element you can't put your finger on but which is omnipresent and creates an environment that is welcoming and nurturing. It's something that is paramount for a restaurant with no menu.

What I do know is that we can't afford to ease up, we need to be hungry to do better each and every day. We can't lose the urgency to keep getting better and better.

Gourmet Traveller is sending a photographer today to shoot some images for the upcoming review. They are quite specific in what they want to shoot and I've gotten rid of a few of the dishes they have asked for. Not out of dislike this time, they were just proving a little hard to plate during the busier services.

I'll just have to spend the morning getting them ready, which is ok, we can just run them tonight. We only have sixteen booked.

The shoot is done and dusted, quick and painless, now all there is to do is sit and wait. I don't know when the issue comes out, but I know I'll think about it until it does.

Today we had restaurant royalty in for lunch, print lifers Terry Durack and Jill Dupleix. Food writers, reviewers and publishers, they are responsible for the *Financial Review* peer-voted 100 Best Restaurants in Australia list, a list I doubt we will ever make, and this year's is due out in just a few weeks.

It was nice to see and cook for them in our new home, and we had a great service. Surprisingly, I was happy with the dishes, which is rarely the case. I am always nit picking the details even if the problems are all in my own head. We were lucky to get a small tray of sun-ripened blackberries, figs from one of the oldest trees on the Bellarine, and grapes that taste like passionfruit from a neighbour. Everyone today was happy, smiling.

We started with a new snack and a series of tarts as well. Abalone, seared quickly on the grill, thinly sliced and served cold with cultured cream and black garlic. Amish paste tomatoes, blanched, tossed in olive oil and salt and left above the grill to dehydrate with a mustard emulsion and tiny mustard leaves, and finally, parmesan custard with aged and cured Cape Barron goose.

Three small bites of land and sea.

> It's days like today, services that make you grow as a restaurant and a team, just a little bit. Days when you can see through all the self-doubt, financial concerns and worries that come with running your own restaurant and when you get a glimpse, just a little ounce of light at what can seem like an endless dark tunnel. They feel good.

Today we have James Viles coming down from Biota in the hinterlands of New South Wales. He is coming to cook with us, the second of our guest chefs, and he tells me how excited he is to be cooking over the fire, experimenting with dishes and techniques he doesn't get to use in his conventional kitchen. It gets everyone in the kitchen excited to share our space with him and his head chef, Nico.

I nervously cooked for them last night. I know it wasn't as good as it should have been. It's nagging at me now, and I almost feel a little embarrassed. It's distracting me, and I can feel myself retreating into my own world, away from the noise and action of the kitchen.

I let James take control. I'm just happy to sit back and watch and let the boys work with James, see his style and learn from him. Today it's his kitchen.

We spent the late hours last night climbing trees, picking leaves and branches for the lunch today, discussing the fire and what produce we have. James is another chef who prefers to interact with produce and ingredients before deciding what to do with them. James, however, is far more organised than I am and already has a plan for tomorrow.

> I'm really looking forward to eating and seeing what he creates, seeing what comes from the fire, another cook's reaction to it, learning a little and having a laugh—the way cooking should be. I've gotta try harder to remember that.

James has started to roast the ducks over the fire and has covered them with the pepper leaves we picked last night to create a smokey oven of sorts, a technique I hadn't considered before. He has essentially created an oven on top of the fire, and I like it. The room is filled with an aroma of sweet pepper, which is another aspect I hadn't considered before we opened: the smell of a fire and how comforting that can be.

James has fallen in love with the fire, with its ability and potential. He's examining its every detail and is now determined to retrofit his kitchen to accommodate one for himself.

The lunch is a hit, with a room full of happy guests standing around chatting to each other like old friends. I point out to James it's just like camping, everyone standing around the fire, drink in hand, telling stories, each one more outrageous than the last. It's the same feeling we experienced at the last meal we did together, a wild lunch out in the forest in New South Wales. It has been a good day, and it's such a nice way to finish the week.

the second review

Fucking hell, please, not tonight, not this week. I'm tired; I can't seem to sleep. The weather over the weekend hasn't been great—100-km winds and 40-degree days—and as a result the produce is ruined, with everything either having been wind-blown or sunburnt. That's February in Victoria for you—unpredictable and a nightmare for me.

I haven't spent a lot on produce because we can't really afford to. The first three weeks have been a little quieter than expected so I'm trying to watch every dollar and make the most out of everything we have in house. We have been finding ways to use everything—broths from leftover carcasses and dried fish bones, sauces from the juice of old vegetables—all within the challenge of not repeating what I've done before, stopping myself from taking the easy way out, and forcing myself onto the edge instead.

So, naturally, it happens to be tonight—this week of all the goddamn weeks—the first major state newspaper food reviewer comes in to dine. What makes things even worse, once again we don't have many people booked. It's another quiet night, one of those nights that it's costing us more to be open, but ok, even more reason to do a great job. Word of mouth, reviews, they all add up and they all help.

Deep breath, here we go…

8 pm

The dining room feels like it has a weird vibe to it, or maybe that's just me. It most likely is. I'm pacing in front of the service bench like a madman, trying to bring the energy in the kitchen up. Everyone is on high alert, but I quickly remind myself that we are all on show, slow myself down to a concentrated panic and try to put this adrenaline to good use.

It's not that we do anything differently for reviewers, it's just that you want to make sure you are doing the very best you can to show and advertise what your little world can do—one chance to get it right, or as close to it as you can.

I turn to the kitchen and say again, 'Don't fuck this up,' but ultimately I know it's all on me if we do.

I know I don't want to serve the same dishes that we served to *Gourmet Traveller*. It's just a thing I have, scared of the written comparisons, I guess, but there are still a few dishes hanging around. It was easier this week, with fewer guests and more time to get myself sorted—maybe I've just been in a better head space—plus I actually like them (it's rare I ever do). They are 'the hits', as I jokingly call them.

Drew has convinced me, as only Drew can, to add the society garlic potatoes to the reviewer's menu. I'm nervous about it, par-cooked potato noodles using five different types of garlic ranging from cultured green garlic butter to dried elephant garlic, herbs, leaves and flowers. It's a pungent dish, but hey, that's garlic for you so why make excuses or try and hide it.

I'm not entirely sure how the noodles will go down—I like them but then again what do I know?—long strands of King Edward potatoes washed in cold running water until the starch runs out then blanched quickly to neutralise the chalkiness raw potatoes can have. The result is a smooth, creamy noodle but still with all the texture and crunch of a raw potato. It was a last-minute dish before we opened, an effort to placate the vegetarians if any were to pop up unannounced.

It's a nervous, shaky start to the night. I don't think anyone expected the attention, definitely not this early on. I know I didn't. I was too busy convincing myself no one would come, no one would be interested in what I was doing in the backstreets of Geelong.

Some days I barely cared, so why would anyone else?

But here they are, and here we are. I have a feeling this isn't going to go well.

the third review

I still haven't slept, not more than an hour or two at a time anyway. A hundred questions and concerns keep me up every night, in addition to plaguing my thoughts during the day. Are we doing all we can to be the best we can be with what we have? Have we nailed what we set out to be? What exactly did we set out to be? Is that a question that I can even answer? Is it a question that even needs answering?

The space still feels awkward. We haven't got to know each other yet—the staff and I, front of house and back of house. And we are on display 100 per cent of the time. There's nowhere to hide here in this box, this claustrophobic coffin I've built for myself. I have felt myself slip, my mood depressed with no energy, no desire to even do this.

> There is nowhere to stop and catch my breath in this restaurant, just me in the middle of four walls, exposed.

There is an upside, though. I can see everything all of the time. It creates an environment that can be open and inviting, or, if we are not careful, hostile. In a split second a misstep in service can be seen, and I'm watching, ready to pounce on the smallest forgotten detail. I have a way of looking at someone, I'm told, that makes my disapproval immediately apparent.

I'm sitting in our closet-sized office, which doubles as a change room, taking five minutes to gather my thoughts from the day. Just a few quiet minutes to decipher what went wrong last night or at the very least figure out what went right, anxiously sifting through yesterday's actions and reactions, wondering was it *any good*? No one really knows yet; we are all still a little shell-shocked. Was the sequence of dishes ok? Did it all make sense? How did the potato noodles go down? I looked at the plates before the dishwasher pounced, they were all clean, but were we attentive enough, or was it too much; did we do enough to create an experience for our guests, and did they like it? Was the room too brightly lit, and how was the temperature? Too hot? Too cold? Just right? Does it matter? Did everyone have clean aprons? Over and over I question and argue with myself, full of self-doubt and concerned whether or not we hit the mark, or survived the review at all.

It's then I hear Drew's voice, loud and thunderous as it can be in times of fear and excitement.

Oh fuck… NO, NO, NO, not again, Jesus Christ no, there is no way this can be happening. Our second national reviewer is standing outside taking a photo of our sign.

Please no! Not again, not today.

You get one chance to get it right, with any guest.

I heard it loud and clear, 'New South Wales, I think.' New South Wales *I think*? What the fuck? Jesus Christ, no, you can't be serious, the spirit our reviewer is drinking is from Adelaide, South Australia not New South Wales. And with that I presume we are fucked, the first step in service—the pre-dinner drink—has been fucked up, and in my head we are done, tripped at the first hurdle. We have totally screwed it up! We haven't even had the chance to serve any food yet, let alone explain how it all works.

How can any of our guests trust us if their very first encounter, their very first interaction with us, isn't right? How will they ever trust us when we stumble right off the bat? It may seem like a small detail, but to me service is won or lost in them.

I feel immediately defeated, my already dark, depressed mood is darkened beyond return.

I am so mad at this stupid mistake. I can't see past it, grinding my teeth to direct my frustration somewhere, my breath shortens and chest tightens, though deep down I know if we are ever going survive I have to gather myself, let it all go and try to redeem the night.

The dishes are the same as last night, with no bag of tricks to dig into, no hidden dishes waiting to make the menu board, no masterstrokes waiting for the exact right moment before they come to life. Nope, we will have to repeat from last night, something I really don't want to do but have little choice. It's my own doing, which frustrates me further.

> One of the most uncomfortable times for me as a cook is watching a guest take the first bite of a dish. Watching, holding a suspended breath for a moment too long, waiting for a reaction, something, anything—a smile, a nod, a wince, some sort of guide to their disgust or enjoyment. As our reviewer busily moves about in his chair, arranging the table, ready for his first taste of IGNI, as the snacks hit the table, I close my eyes, turn my head and look away. I can't watch this.

We have come to the fifth course, the final savoury a fourteen-day aged squab. We can't get this wrong.

I call from the pass, 'Away on two squab.' 'Yes Chef,' is the answer.

I turn to Jono, in charge of the grill. 'Cook four if you have to. I'll take the centre cuts only, and plate from there. Just don't fuck it up, please.'

The protein needs to be ever-so-slightly set, a firm jelly-like texture, deep red in colour, consistent throughout with crisp roasted skin. It's a bird that requires absolute attention from start to finish. I have forgiven it being a little overcooked previously due to the newness of cooking over fire but not this time, no way.

Jono nails it, the squab is done perfectly and for a moment I can breathe easy, knowing that at least one of the dishes tonight will hit the mark. In a moment of reflection I remember it being one of the dishes that truly has the IGNI stamp, simple and seasonal.

Drew is also convinced that he has fucked it up—a misspelled wine on the list is irritating him, compounding his self-doubt. I mention the spirit incident to him and we both just look at each other in shock and start to laugh nervously. I wasn't going to have a drink tonight, but fuck it, I need one to calm the anxiety.

Who serves par-cooked potato as a penultimate savoury course? Aaron Turner. And damned if you won't be downing tools and throwing hands in the air. In the hands of the chef who made onion ice-cream a thing at Loam, now shuttered, but winner of *The Age Good Food Guide*'s Regional Restaurant of the Year in 2012, the humble spud is transformed into aglio e olio with extra crunch. Al dente shoelaces are cooked in their own starchy water, and tossed with the infused oil plus crisp-fried discs and flowers of society garlic. Pretty, complex—it's an underdog dish for the ages.

Serious eaters have spent the past two years awaiting the return of Turner's simple-yet-mindblowing combinations that celebrate ingredients for what they are. They've had his Nashville hot chicken to tide them over at the Hot Chicken Project on Little Malop Street. But it's Turner's innate ability to read flavour, see new possibilities in flavour combinations that are not insane, that's been missed. Fans hoped, but weren't sure, if the easy, natural essence of Loam could translate from an olive grove in Drysdale to the rear of a Bikram studio in Geelong.

They can now exhale.

There are two butternut pumpkins sitting on the bench that have turned up at some point, no one seems to know where they came from or who brought them in. I just keep moving them around the restaurant, out of my way, assuming someone will collect them and take them to their intended purpose at some point. I have a strong dislike for pumpkin, in fact I hate them, so I have no inkling to do anything with them. I've never liked them, subjected to years of them steamed within an inch of their life, the texture fibrous and mushy. Come to think of it, I distrust most orange vegetables—sweet potato and cooked carrots, no thanks.

I've moved the pumpkins around the restaurant in the hope they will find their rightful home. They have gone from the kitchen to the office to the bar to the dry store and, finally, into a tote at the bottom of the cool room. They don't seem to have a home, these mystery pumpkins.

So today I decided to do something with them. I've decided to put them on the grill when the fire is burning slowly, almost smouldering, during mid-afternoon, basting them with oil and butter as the day goes on, moving them every so often to the hottest part of the grill.

Nothing has really happened by the time we need to stoke the fire for service; there are a few light-coloured grill marks, but I think nothing of it, put them in the cool room and forget about them. Maybe they will have a use tomorrow, for staff meal perhaps.

Jono asked about the pumpkins in the cool room—he's giving it a deep clean and is curious whether or not we are keeping them. I'm really not sure, I explain, I guess so. I'll just keep repeating today's process every day once the fire has burned down from the morning prep, until something happens. What, exactly, I'm not sure... maybe slowly roasting them will concentrate the sugars, draw out the earthy sweetness, or they may just burn on the outside, stew in the middle and taste like shit, but let's see what happens.

That was a week I could happily forget, or at least re-do: two of Australia's premier restaurant reviewers came unexpectedly through the doors on consecutive nights, and the restaurant just isn't ready for the attention, not yet. Maybe in six months, but that's a grace period we just don't get. I knew that, deep down. Not feeling ready, that's on me. I should have pushed harder.

We are lucky they are even paying attention to what we are doing down here in this back alley, we just aren't ready. In no way are we what we want to be, a cohesive unit, a restaurant comfortable in its own ability.

Now it's a waiting game, a game of chance. We have rolled our dice and we wait, and wait for the reviews to come in, stomach firmly in throats.

In truth I'm nervous, but calmer than I thought I would be, resigned to the fact the reviews won't be great because I'm sure we fucked it up. But on the other hand I hope we haven't. We need a positive review; they can make a huge difference to a restaurant off the beaten track. I've been the beneficiary before and right now, let's face it, we need that. Bookings are slow.

society garlic potatoes

Washing the potatoes to remove the excess starch and then briefly cooking them results in a finished texture similar to that of the raw vegetable. At IGNI we like to finish them with society garlic flowers, wild onion, dried organic garlic and leek ash, but you can add anything you like—anchovies, jamon or loads of freshly grated parmesan all work well.

4 king edward potatoes, washed and peeled
1 tablespoon salt
1 tablespoon grapeseed oil
2 tablespoons Freshly churned butter (page 124),
    at room temperature
1 garlic clove, minced
1 lemon wedge or a splash of aged vinegar

to serve (optional)

anchovies
jamon
freshly grated parmesan

serves 4

Cut the potatoes into long continuous noodles using a spiral cutter.

Wash the potato noodles thoroughly in a bowl of fresh running water until the water changes to a light bronze colour and begins to foam slightly.

Fill a large saucepan with equal quantities of the potato water and regular cold water. Add the salt and potato noodles, bring to a simmer and cook for 5 minutes, or until the noodles are al dente. Drain the potato noodles and refresh in a bowl of ice-cold water.

Warm a little grapeseed oil in a non-stick frying pan, add the butter and heat until it begins to froth, then add the garlic and cook, stirring, until golden.

Drain the potato noodles, then add them to the pan and toss until coated. Squeeze over the lemon juice and season with salt, then add your choice of flavourings to finish. Divide among plates and serve.

hay-smoked duck

As well as being all about the exceptional pekin duck that we are lucky to get from Great Ocean Ducks, this dish needs the right sort of hay— not the pet shop kind but the sticky, treacly sort that is full of wild grasses, dried flowers and natural oils, which help to impart a beautiful, earthy flavour both when the duck is smoking and during the hanging and ageing process.

1 x 2–3 kg (4 lb 6 ox–6 lb 10 oz) good-quality duck, stuffed with hay and hung for 14 days
2 handfuls of dried hay
hot embers

serves 6

Wash the duck and pat dry, then remove the legs and thighs with a sharp knife, being careful to leave as much skin as possible around the breast. Set aside at room temperature on a wire rack.

Lay the hay over the base of a deep tray, piling it up at one end. Drop a hot ember in the middle of the hay pile and cover with the remaining hay. Place the wire rack with the duck on top of the smoking hay and cover with a second deep tray to create a sealed environment.

Leave to smoke for 6 minutes, then repeat the process twice more, replacing the hay and embers as you go. Remove the duck from the smoker and leave to chill.

When ready to cook, set the duck on a grill over a fire and cook, moving it around in the flames, until the skin is crisp and golden. Turn the duck breast-side up and transfer it to the side of the fire to finish cooking (this should take about 15 minutes). Carve and serve.

young pepper/pickled strawberries

While I don't have a sweet tooth, I love ice cream. In the same way that most chefs love making bread, it's the process that I find really enjoyable. We always have a few (with varying degrees of sweetness) on the menu at IGNI. After the fire and smoke of the rest of the food they feel like a pretty, fresh way to finish a meal.

The centre of Geelong is full of old pepper trees, the result of a council planting initiative a while back no doubt, and the young leaves for this ice cream come from the massive established tree by the church on my way to work. Full of essential oils, the leaves have a delicate, peppery flavour when fresh that intensifies when dried out.

young pepper leaves, dehydrated and finely ground, to serve

ice cream

275 g (9½ oz) goat's milk
250 g (9 oz) jersey cream
80 g (2¾ oz) young pepper leaves
7 egg yolks
220 g (8 oz/1 cup) sugar

pickled strawberries

250 g (9 oz) strawberries
2 tablespoons caster (superfine) sugar
splash of rice vinegar
½ bunch shiso leaves

serves 4–6

For the ice cream, warm the milk and cream in a saucepan over a medium heat. Stir in the pepper leaves, cover and infuse in the fridge overnight.

The next day, whisk the egg yolks and sugar together in a bowl until pale and fluffy. Warm the milk and cream infusion in the saucepan to 88°C (190°F) then carefully strain, removing the pepper leaves. Pour over the egg mixture, beating slowly, until cooled, then transfer to the refrigerator to chill before pouring into an ice cream machine and churning until frozen. Keep in the freezer until needed.

For the pickled strawberries, roughly chop half the strawberries and add them to a bowl with the sugar and 70 ml (2 1/4 fl oz) water. Cover with plastic wrap and set over a saucepan of simmering water for 20 minutes, until the berries are pale and the liquid surrounding them is bright red. Add the rice vinegar then strain, discarding the solids, and leave to cool.

Once cool, place the liquid in a blender with the shiso leaves and blitz together on high for 2 minutes. Pass through a fine sieve.

Cut the remaining strawberries into fingernail-sized pieces and place in a container. Pour over the strained liquid and set aside until needed.

To serve, add a tablespoon of strawberries to each bowl with a scoop of ice cream, a sprinkle of pepper powder and a splash of pickle liquid.

march

I've been nursing the pumpkins all week, subjecting them to a low heat for a couple of hours each day, rolling them around the grill and chasing the hot spots as the embers flare and die off. I've basted them with whatever fats we have rendered, giving them a pinch of salt here and there, more out of function than anything.

The outside skin, the parts as an apprentice you would dread having to cut off, have blackened to the deepest glossy black I think I've ever seen on a vegetable. I still have no idea what I'll do with them and what the insides will look or taste like. The experiment might have been a huge waste of time but I'm eager to find out.

Today we have Roger and Sue coming in for lunch, importers of natural wine and contributors to *Gourmet Traveller* magazine. I've known them for years, long before natural wine was ever a thing, when they were importing just a couple of different wines out of pure love and joy. It's been a while since they have eaten my food, three or more years if I had to guess, and I'm nervous what they will think. I wish I still had more time to get better at this, to have better dishes and a better understanding of what I'm trying to do.

I'm pretty sure I've picked the last of the wild blackberries from the coast, not quite as ripe as perhaps they were a few weeks ago when they were bursting from the summer's sun. But now they're sweet and sour and a nice representation of a wild berry late in its short season.

Rowan cooked and picked the spanner crab this morning, again with no real plan of what to do with it, we just managed to get our hands on three live ones from Lucas, our fish guy, early Saturday morning. I'm desperately trying to figure something out—there are about fifteen portions of sweet translucent crabmeat we just have to use.

I've been fermenting a blend of rye, barley and buckwheat in a mixture of equal parts fresh goat's milk and acidic goat's whey with marjoram and fresh oregano. When they sour about fourteen days later the grains are cooked quickly, finished off in a stock of fresh herbs and vegetables.

Texturally it will be a nice contrast to the silky crab, each grain popping with each mouthful—an acidic, lactic taste of the ocean that sounds good to me.

I'll serve it and cross my fingers it works out.

6 pm

It turns out the pumpkin wasn't great, not a complete waste of time, just not great. The flesh still tasted exactly like steamed pumpkin, but puréed whole—seeds, flesh and blackened skin—with enough butter we ended up with a smokey pumpkin butter of sorts. It wasn't a complete failure but not something I'll quickly repeat with pumpkin, but I wonder how other vegetables might behave? A thought for another day.

There's a sharp rhythmic noise coming from my phone, charging on my bedside table. I grab at it only for it to smash onto the ground, still tethered to the wall. I can barely read it through blurry, pre-coffee eyes, but I make out that someone up much earlier than me is reading a review of our little restaurant. I knew it was coming today, I just didn't want to read it. I'd actually done pretty well at ignoring the fact that it was coming out today. I see the score sticking out of the message—16/20. I don't bother reading the rest of the message, just roll over and go back to sleep.

I still haven't picked up a newspaper or searched online to read the review. In fact, I've done everything I can to distract myself from it. I'm in a bad mood before I've even read it; I know there will be comparisons to Loam. I wish there weren't, but that's just the way it is. Still, I'm worried about it—is it positive, does it dig up the past, are we doing a good job? Because it really doesn't feel like it yet, and I definitely don't want to read about it if we aren't. I know we should be better; the opening should have been stronger.

Just seven weeks after opening and here is our first printed review on sale, out there for everybody and anybody to read.

Mum has called and before I can say anything she's started to read the review over the phone. I hold it in the air away from my ear so I can't hear what she's saying. She gets mad and tells me not to be stupid and to read it, that it's great.

I've finally picked up a copy of the paper and a six-pack of beer just in case, at least I can drink my way through if needs be. I sit down to read the first line…

…Who serves par-cooked potato?

I sink, frozen, stuck. I try and take a swill of beer only I'm too frightened to move, convincing myself that if I don't read it everything will be ok, the words will disappear.

I knew I fucked it up.

I force myself to keep reading the next line.

….and damned if you won't be downing tools and throwing hands in the air…

…it's an underdog dish for the ages…

My body collapses in relief.

The rest of the review reads well, really well, and if I'm honest it's better than we deserve at this stage. I'm so relieved that in under two months we have been lucky enough to survive and receive such a great review.

It gives me the resolve to do better, but also makes me worry that I can't, that I got lucky this time. These expectations can weigh heavily at times and I'm not as strong as I used to be. I used to not give a fuck.

I know we have a lot of work to do, it's just a matter of finding the will and energy to do it.

Tomorrow I resolve to begin again from the start. The bar has been raised and now we have to rise to meet it.

above: tuna tail

That's an odd name. Jo seems to remember it being one of James Spader's character's names on a TV show, and her research hasn't come up with any intel, except to confirm this fact.

I brush it off as a coincidence; I'm a little distracted. It's a quiet lunch and the mood is quite low. I'm struggling to keep everyone focused and upbeat and again trying to change the energy in the room, something that's hard to do when the number of staff outweighs the number of guests.

There's a small opening in the blinds that I watch like a hawk for incoming guests. The reflection in the mirror helps me see the other way too.

We've been missing our guests at the door recently. This is the very first interaction our guests have with IGNI after the booking process, which Drew is working hard to perfect. So why aren't we putting equal importance on greeting our guests once they actually arrive? With that in mind this week I'm riding everyone about not missing this step. It's a constant battle to get this first step in service right.

Service has started and just kind of mumbles along, as if nothing at all. It's another quiet Saturday lunch with only twelve guests and most of them are doing just five courses, which makes the space feel overstaffed. The ratio of staff to diners seems off, but we will need them trained and ready once or if we ever get busy.

It's then, a brief second later when I look up through the crack in the blinds, that I see a face I know. It's the head restaurant and national restaurant reviewer and crew from *Gourmet Traveller* on their way down the alley and in the doors of IGNI.

Oh shit, not again. Here we go.

By now the kitchen crew know exactly the state of urgency this creates. Almost immediately upon explanation their attention turns to red alert, it's like a jolt of electricity shoots through the restaurant and all of a sudden we are alive, awake, running on full steam, alert and ready to go. I can't help wondering why we aren't always like this.

'Ok, so what are we feeding them? Rowan, what have you got? Jono check the pigeon... NOW!'

Thankfully, we have three pigeon left—it seems like the go-to dish for our food reviewers. We have been carefully nurturing and aging them in dried grasses and hay. You don't see them on many menus in Australia—they are price prohibitive for the most part—but they're one of my favourite things to cook and to share with guests, so I always have them around in some form or another.

There's pretty much no one left in the dining room, which is both bad and good. Bad that there isn't a vibe, which means it feels very strange and sterile, good because we can focus all our attention on the table. It does make it a little awkward, an empty restaurant and them sitting alone while we go about our business. I'm sure the first question they are asking is, 'Why isn't anyone here?'

And it's then, in a hot flush of anxiety, I realise that if we do indeed fuck this up, there will be no excuses, nothing to blame our poor performance on, no reasoning away the fact that we didn't get it right. I try to outsmart the creeping fear, the sudden drop in energy and tell myself, stop, just stop being scared. Stop the sabotage and just cook, Aaron, for fuck's sake just cook.

I snap back and find myself plating the spanner crab and fermented grains. It looks ugly. Let's be honest, it looks like vomit. A bowl of white silky crab, coated in a fawn-coloured porridge—a mix of grains that looks like the result of a big night out. Horrifying. I've tried in vain to make it look a little more appealing but failed, so here it is—a small bowl, a few mouthfuls of last night's party that's about to be served to our reviewer. Maybe not a smart move, but it's all I've got and it tastes good, I think, though at this point I'm starting to question even that.

There seems to be a lot of banter on the table, nothing that indicates that the experience at IGNI is worth mentioning. I feel bad. I feel like I've failed, and I can't shake this feeling of failure.

I should have never tried; I should have stayed away from cooking, from everything.

I am not having fun.

21·03·2016

2 am

There's a message on my phone I have just seen, sent two hours ago, a link to the *Gourmet Traveller* restaurant review site, a photo of Jo, Drew and I standing in the doorway of IGNI.

The title: Man on Fire.

I agree. I feel on fire, burning with expectations, my own more than anyone else's.

I don't get past the first paragraph. I'm in no mood—too many dead bodies, ex-wives, and ghost stories for my tired brain to make sense of. I'll read it in the morning.

22·03·2016

I'll read it, I promised myself I would. The first visit from *Gourmet Traveller*, a summary of the very first Sunday service we were open, good bad or otherwise. It is what it is, no amount of hope or voodoo can or will change what's written, so here I go...

I'm not sure if it's relief, or the constant mention of past lives, but I break down and start to cry.

'A return to cooking and better than ever...'

Kind words I'm convinced aren't accurate.

above: goolwa pippies

above: fermented cabbage

Well, I've just stabbed myself. Once again I'm off in my own head, a million miles from where I'm supposed to be, which is cleaning radicchio, and suddenly and without warning the turning knife takes on a life of its own and slips around the core. Fuck me, there's a knife sticking out of my hand. *Calm down, calm down.* Except I've never done this before, so I'm freaking out.

I mean, I've cut myself before, but not actually stabbed myself. I've never had a knife sticking into or out of a body part before and it fucking hurts.

In what seems like seconds I pull the knife out as a reflex action, throw it on the floor and cover the wound with my other hand, but by now it's pulsing blood all over the place. Rowan squeals, 'That's gonna need stitches, Chef,' and I shoot him a look of disdain. 'What the fuck? No it won't. Just get me some paper towels and I'll be fine.'

> I look down and pull my hand holding the wound away to see what damage I've done. I can see the inside of my palm folding out of my skin. It's pulsating blood into the air and running down my arm.

Yep, that's gonna need stitches.

The emergency room is the usual affair, tired doctors and nurses doing the best they can after endless hours of dealing with the injured public and budget cuts. A student doctor with no experience to speak of has started to clean me up; he reminds me of an apprentice chef nervously butchering a cut of meat for the first time. It's awkward to watch.

The student doctor and his supervisor are busily poking around in the wound to find the tip of the knife they are convinced is in there. The pain is beginning to be a little unbearable and when I tell them my fingers are going numb the student doctor suddenly remembers she forgot to localise the area. It's not until a few painkillers are administered that I start to relax and watch what feels like a thousand needles piercing my skin. The stitches have begun.

Wide-eyed and dry-mouthed they continue to poke and prod at me for what seems like hours until they finally finish, bandage me up and send me back to work.

With a crooked smile and eyes as wide as my face (the painkillers have set in) I start the walk back from emergency to the restaurant, having to sit every hundred metres or so to settle my light head and contemplate why the world looks so bright and the birds are singing so loud. I have no idea how I'm going to get through service, and knowing my luck a reviewer will come through our doors. I have one good hand and I'm completely spaced out, my mouth's a little dry and I feel like sleeping, yet for some strange reason all I can think about is seaweed. It gives me an idea for a dish, I think? I write it down.

octopus
octopus
seaweed and fish

What the hell is that that I've scribbled in my note book? *Octopus, octopus seaweed and fish*?

Now that the painkillers have worn off it sounds like the name of a kid's book (note: pitch it to the publisher). My hand is bruised and swollen, the upside being that thanks to the painkillers I finally slept a full night, the first time in a long while.

I still feel like shit and the pain is more than real as it turns out I hit the bone with the tip of my knife. I'm pretty useless, so I have no choice but to hand over the kitchen to the boys. Perhaps it's a good thing. I'll be able to observe for the day and for the first time ever in a kitchen I've run and owned, I'll let them take the wheel. I convince myself I don't really care and that maybe this is a good thing, that for my own sanity this had to happen.

> Today is the last day before the Easter close. We can't really afford the break to pay staff and rent with no income coming into the restaurant but we all agreed before opening that we would take these holidays. We need the break to have at least a little sense of being part of the outside world. It's six days to switch off and attempt to live a normal, balanced life. That's the goal of IGNI—balance. Though I still wonder what that is.

It's hard, trying to find a balance when opening or running a restaurant. Your attention has to be on everything, all the time. There's the focus on trying to get it right every single service, hoping to improve just a little every day. Then there's the cash flow, another tricky balance, and the first three months are crucial. You are usually out of capital because it's all been spent on the unforeseen events that come with turning an empty box into a restaurant—there's the little things like more pots and pans needed for the kitchen, more glassware to replace the ones that have broken, then there's the big things like the water pressure that turns out isn't quite adequate—so there's a thousand dollars you haven't budgeted for—as well as a few surprises no one saw coming like the air conditioning needing an upgrade. The list goes on and on and on until you're at least a third over the original budget, while issues with staff and suppliers, unhinged dishwashers and tantrums from everyone help fill up the days and the weeks.

We have only been open just over eight weeks but I've had enough and am ready for a break. I'm still not sure if I can get this done. If I can continue to survive this return to cooking.

above: Blake Coster

spanner crab/fermented grains

We rely so heavily on the visual when it comes to eating that I really struggled with serving this dish, fighting against that need to make everything look pretty and trying everything I could to make it look more appealing. In the end though, flavour won out.

1 x 400 g (14 oz) live spanner crab

fermented grains

200 g (7 oz) goat's milk
200 g (7 oz) acidic goat's whey
100 g (3½ oz) sheep's yoghurt
20 g (¾ oz) sugar
100 g (3½ oz) rye
100 g (3½ oz) millet
100 g (3½ oz) barley
6 oregano sprigs
4 fresh bay leaves
½ bunch thyme
½ bunch tarragon
1 litre (34 fl oz/4 cups) light chicken stock

serves 4

For the fermented grains, combine the goat's milk, goat's whey and yoghurt together in a bowl and whisk in the sugar.

Put the grains in a separate large bowl, pour over the goat's milk mixture and add the oregano, then cover with muslin and leave to ferment on a bench at a stable room temperature for 4–7 days, or until a skin has formed on top of the grain mix. The grains will start to smell bready when fermentation has begun. If mould appears on top of the mix then scrape it off.

When ready to cook, tie the rest of the herbs together with string and place in a large saucepan. Scrape the skin off the fermented grain mix and add the grains to the pan, cover with the chicken stock and leave to simmer gently until the grains are al dente. Keep warm.

Meanwhile, bring a large saucepan of water to a rapid boil, add the crab and cover with plastic wrap. Remove from the heat and leave to sit for 35 minutes, then remove the crab from the pan and leave to cool. Once cool, pick all the meat from the shell, being careful not to leave any behind.

To serve, divide the grain mix among bowls and spoon over the freshly picked crab meat.

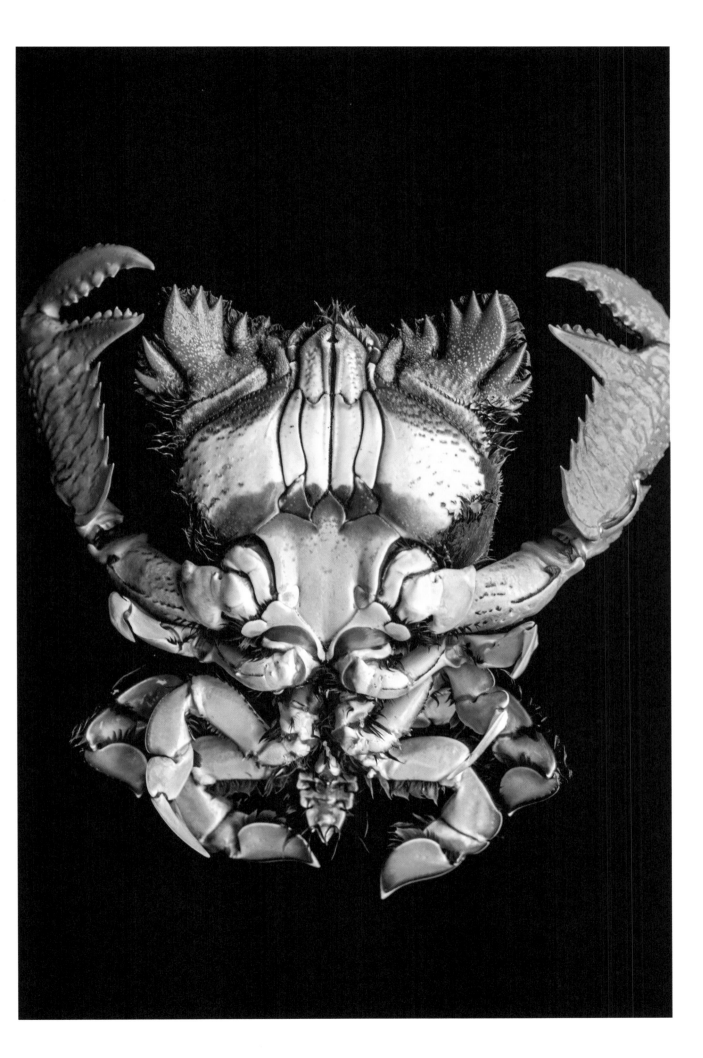

raw cuttlefish/celeriac/lemon/wild fennel

When cuttlefish are at their best and in peak condition there is no better way to serve them than raw. This whole dish is about texture and relies on every ingredient being at its best.

1 x 200 g (7 oz) cuttlefish
1 bunch parsley, leaves only
50 g (1¾ oz) wild fennel
1 celeriac, peeled

lemon emulsion

juice of 2 lemons
pinch of white pepper
1 egg
1 teaspoon dijon mustard
200 ml (7 fl oz) grapeseed oil
salt flakes

serves 4–6

To prepare the cuttlefish, remove the stomach by holding the head in one hand and the tube in the other and slowly pulling in opposite directions. Remove the wings by pinching your thumb and forefinger at the base and pulling away from the body. Use a dry kitchen cloth to wipe the cuttlefish tube clean, making sure to remove the outer film, then open the tube by slicing down the centre. Wash the tube thoroughly, then slice in half lengthways. Stack the two tube halves on top of each other, wrap in plastic wrap and freeze.

For the lemon emulsion, add the lemon juice, white pepper, egg and mustard to a blender and blitz together on high, gradually adding the grapeseed oil until the mixture has thickened slightly. Season with salt to taste.

Dehydrate the parsley and wild fennel on the lowest setting of a dehydrator, then transfer to a spice grinder and blitz to a powder.

Slice the celeriac into long ribbons using a mandoline.

Plate as you wish.

seaweed/quinoa

Before IGNI opened I cooked for a dinner in Melbourne with some friends from Sydney's Pinbone restaurant. I didn't really know what to do that night but I was in charge of dessert, so I threw this together and hoped for the best. It went down a storm, with one of the chefs approaching me afterwards and insisting it should be on the menu when we opened. The best sort of happy accident.

100 g (3½ oz) quinoa
pinch of salt flakes

ice cream

3 dried seaweed sheets (such as nori)
275 g (9½ oz) goat's milk
250 g (9 oz) jersey cream
7 egg yolks
220 g (8 oz/1 cup) sugar

seaweed sugar

3 dried seaweed sheets (such as nori)
40 g (1½ oz) matcha powder
80 g (2¾ oz) icing (confectioners') sugar

serves 4–6

For the ice cream, roast the seaweed sheets over a fire until crisp. Warm the milk and cream in a saucepan over a medium heat. Add the seaweed sheets, cover and leave to infuse overnight in the fridge.

The next day, whisk the egg yolks and sugar together in a bowl until pale and fluffy. Warm the milk and cream infusion in the saucepan to 88°C (190°F) then carefully strain, removing the nori sheets. Pour over the egg mixture, beating slowly, until cooled, then transfer to the refrigerator to chill before pouring into an ice cream machine and churning until frozen. Keep in the freezer until needed.

Preheat an oven to 150°C (300°F/Gas 2).

Add the quinoa and salt to a saucepan with 600 ml (20½ fl oz) water and simmer until the quinoa is soft and overcooked and the water has almost evaporated. Transfer to a blender and blitz on high to form a purée. Spread the mixture out over a baking tray in a thin, even layer and cook in the oven for 15 minutes, or until golden and crisp.

For the seaweed sugar, roast the seaweed sheets over a fire until crisp, then add them to a blender with the remaining ingredients and blitz to combine. Pass though a fine sieve.

Plate as you wish.

april

above: beurre bosc pear
opposite: wild scampi roe

Today is, I think, the biggest night we have had yet, bookings-wise. I'm sure someone is playing a joke on me, it being April Fool's and all. We have thirty-three guests booked on a Friday night. Up till now it's averaged eighteen or so, so for us that's a full house.

The rest of the coming week is looking pretty solid too, which comes as a relief. After a few very quiet weeks and having closed for the Easter break the little cash surplus we had in reserve has been eaten up. The other challenge we have coming this month is a new front-of-house team member starting with us. How we are going to afford it is still a mystery. It will push our labour costs to over 50 per cent, which is completely unsustainable, so we are stuck somewhere in the middle, between needing a fourth full-time front-of-house team member to get better at what we do and hoping we somehow get busier, our bookings increase, our spend per head increases, and we find the magic formula to make the restaurant work.

06·04·2016

Last week was a little busier than we have been, almost full for most dinner services, although lunches were still pretty quiet. I wonder if it is the alley keeping people away, a room without a sprawling view of gardens and groves, instead all you see is just a graffiti-ed, worn-down old brick building.

Over the last couple of weeks the spanner crabs have become increasingly scarce and inconsistent, so I've been planning on changing or using the fermented grains in a different way but with no real success or inspiration so far.

This morning Bruce dropped off a canvas bag of freshly picked mushrooms that have been growing in the paddocks and under the pines on the farm. A tote of odds and ends, not in the best condition, but cleaned up and sorted through I'm sure we will find a use for them.

I'll dehydrate the stalks and trimmings for a later use, a sauce of dried wild mushrooms—or wait, an ice cream perhaps? The mushrooms that are in good enough condition I'll brush clean, ready for when a burst of inspiration hits.

> The mixed bag of spongy slippery jacks, bright orange pines and horse mushrooms smells like wet earth. It's comforting, reminding me to organise a camping trip for when we have a break in June—a getaway, a space to reset, reflect and consider the road ahead. It's something I've never let myself do, always moving forward, no time to rest or take stock.

Merryn, our new team member, is starting to take tables today. It's a quiet night, so things can't go too wrong. It's a strange feeling bringing a new member and a new energy into the team, especially into such a small environment. Working so close together the chemistry has to be right or it is immediately obvious to everyone, especially the guests. Fingers crossed.

09·04·2016

7 am

I didn't want to get out of bed this morning. It would have been easier to just pull the sheets over my head and stay there hiding from the day. Today is the day the review of IGNI will be in the *The Australian*.

It's such a strange feeling reading about yourself, applause or otherwise. It's hard to accept the nice things someone may write, easier to be resolved to do better when they write bad or negative words. I won't read it, not right now; I'll hear all about it, good bad or otherwise, soon enough, so I'll get through the day and take stock of it all later tonight.

4 pm

The mushrooms have made it onto the menu, a dish—risotto, if you like—of fermented grains, a mix of wild mushrooms and cured beef. The mushrooms are gently roasted over red gum and seasoned with a native pepper then folded through a wet mix of fermented grains and brown chicken stock and finished with a mix of dried mushroom powder and thinly sliced cured wagyu, an earthy dish full of the flavours of autumn. Quite a rich dish, and in a strange way reassuring and comforting. I might actually know what I'm doing.

11·45 pm

Four out of five. There it is in print, it can't be wrong. The review I knew we had fucked up is out for everyone to read and I do so with a deep sigh of relief. It is, thankfully, glowing—nicer words than I think we deserve. I'm humbled and relieved. We survived. For reasons I'm not sure of, an incredible sadness washes over me. Perhaps it's relief disguised as something else, I'm not sure.

I'm hoping this might finally kickstart something. We really need the bookings to pick up and be consistent, because even if the reviews continue to be as great as they have been we won't survive, becoming instead just another statistic of restaurant closures.

13·04·2016

Oddly, Wednesdays are turning out to be one of our busiest nights, with us consistently doing the highest number of guests of any service. This is great but also a little concerning given we have decided to close on Wednesdays after the July break. Thursday nights are usually shit, with an average of nine covers, a couple more if we are lucky.

We always wanted IGNI to provide a lifestyle, some sort of work–life balance for everyone. We don't want to get lost in the hospitality life of five double shifts with perhaps a sixth straight to cover someone who is sick or just called out. It's not a lifestyle I want anymore, the years of feeding off an impossible work load. I now know that hospitality has to change—the expectations, the expected hours—it needs to be healthier for everyone involved.

So a decision was made to condense our working lives into six services in four days, reducing our days but actually picking up a service in the process. The new hours are to be Thursday to Saturday dinner with Friday to Sunday lunch, closing Monday and Tuesday while freeing Wednesday for staff development, training, excursions, or simply an extra day off.

On paper this looks like an incredibly stupid move, closing one of the busiest nights in a restaurant not yet three months old. Financially it's suicide, but hey, either you do it or you don't. Simple.

Now cross your fingers and pray it works out.

John Lethlean   *The Australian*   Published 09.04.2016

It starts with a series of snacks. Emu bresaola, cured with cacao powder and dressed with fennel oil; a wafer of lardo-like guanciale, creamy and persistent in the mouth. Sticks of dried, almost candied beef, like unspiced jerky; baby zucchini flowers grilled with just-cooked local mussels inside; whipped cod roe on crisp wafers of chicken skin; salt and vinegar saltbush. And an oyster, warmed in its shell, dressed with a seawater emulsion and oyster plant, a leaf I've not seen before.

Lovely little buns come with hot-smoked, whipped butter. At each turn, these little details are nailed. Another three-element dish of utter simplicity and beauty: batons of fermented baby cucumber with a just-set, grilled piece of marron, all in a pil pil, or crustacean butter. My goodness.

Beets and whey is another three-part harmony: a slice of sweet-yet-savoury roasted beetroot, a layer of nasturtium leaf cooked in some manner, and a lactic moat of gently acidic whey. Each flavour is clear and pure. Charcoal roasted squab leg/thigh, and a piece of rare breast meat in a wild plum sauce, is as pretty as it is desirable. Garnishes of plum, beach succulent and leek ash are almost superfluous, the meat superb and expertly cooked with a lacquered skin, ruby muscle. And it's hot. Have you forgotten what it's like to eat hot meat?

Don't ask how they create noodles of King Edward potato that look like spaghetti in society garlic butter with garlic crisps. The texture is extraordinary, crunchy but soft ... 'Old ewe, new ewe' is a clever little dish of Roquefort with sheep yoghurt granita, the rich flavour of the cheese played off against the fresh, cool acid of the local product.

Fresh local berries and sabayon are intriguingly mixed with icy pellets of lemon curd and berry juices made, presumably, with liquid nitrogen. The effect is superb; quinoa wafers dusted with green tea powder, sandwiching a sticky and sweet seaweed ice cream, is more polarising. But interesting.

Beyond the food, which is almost uniformly excellent and lacks the arrogance so often seen in this kind of place, Turner has created a really hospitable new restaurant. Visit. They'll be pleased to see you.

Today is Sunday, the sky overcast and moody but still warm, and we have four guests booked.

It's disastrous. I feel embarrassed for the guests sitting in an empty restaurant. Today is one of those days where you can't see the path forward, blinded by self-doubt and convinced everything you are doing is complete shit, a worthless waste of time. The phone doesn't ring, there's far too much food in various states of preparation that you know will be wasted, while the wines opened last night will be poured down the sink or at least the throats of thirsty staff.

The financial burden of wages, leases, rents and a million other things that make the bank account dwindle each week, the reality of it all is staring you in the face, mocking you from all the empty tables and chairs.

The only thing I can control today is cancelling the dishwasher, saving a few hours of wages.

It means I'll have to wash the dishes. I'm ok with that, I've done it for most Thursday nights recently and I quite like it. I can hide away in there, away from the awkward tension an empty room brings.

21·04·2016

Tonight we had another reviewer come to visit, this time from *Time Out*, and it's another quiet one, just nine covers. Last night we had twenty-eight guests—six more than the previous Saturday night. Wednesday again is proving to be one of our busiest nights.

> I still wonder if it will ever change. I thought perhaps the review from last week would have set off a wave of reservations but it hasn't, not really, just a small increase of people wanting a table for a Saturday night.

I have spent the last few weeks trying to reduce our already tight weekly budget in the kitchen. I'm worried if I don't we may not have enough money in the bank to pay staff and bills come June when we have scheduled a few weeks' break. But right now our reviewer is here and again I go through the motions, nervously watching every bite, every raised eyebrow or questionable furrow of the forehead, anything to get a read on how they might be enjoying the evening.

I've been struggling to focus lately on changes—on anything really—which makes me a little nervous and compounds the issue further. I know some of the dishes aren't as solid as they can be. It's a realisation of my own disappointment; I could be doing better.

Once again I have no idea how that went. Even if I thought it went well I wouldn't allow myself the luxury of admitting it; instead I'll replay the night in my head, reliving each course, recounting each moment in the hopes of recalling a second of clarity or a moment during service that offers relief from the scorching self-doubt, searching for comfort that somehow allows me to believe everything went ok.

I know it's a waste of time and energy but my head gets stuck in a constant loop, convincing myself I've failed. I nervously recall sending a dessert, one that has promise, maybe.

It isn't quite there yet, I just wanted to send a dish we hadn't sent before, and in a moment of 'fuck it, just send it', we sent our reviewer a dish I'm not completely happy with.

But then again, am I ever?

The dish was a savoury ice cream of slippery jack mushrooms cooked over the fire with sweetened dried apple and a light purée of quince spiked with anise that I had been saving. Drew and Jo are convinced it's delicious but I'm not quite sure. The same thing happened years ago at Loam with a roasted onion ice cream. I liked it but was certain no one else would. It went on to be listed in various publications' Top Dishes of the Year lists. I should take comfort in that, but I don't.

I expected to feel different by now. I've been waiting for the familiar feeling of taking comfort in cooking and of being back in the kitchen— an environment that for the longest time provided a safe haven, somewhere I could just do what I do, whatever that is or was, away from the outside world, a bubble of my own creation. But I don't feel that here. This kitchen still feels as foreign to me as it did three months ago when we opened the doors. I feel like I don't belong here; I'm an intruder, a masked bandit in someone else's house, rummaging through, looking for something, anything of value.

Starting again is hard, let no one ever tell you it's easy.

fermented grains/horse mushroom/cured wagyu

This recipe came about on the fly. We had the fermented grains kicking about in the kitchen already and had been planning to serve them with the spanner crab as usual but there was no supply that week, so my mind turned instead to the mushrooms that Bruce had dropped off earlier that morning complete with a breezy greeting of, 'I assume these are edible'. With the mushrooms grilled over the fire, the end result was uniquely comforting.

2 large horse mushrooms, trimmed and cleaned
clarified butter, for basting
salt flakes and freshly ground black pepper
Fermented grains (see page 98), cooked and kept warm
12 paper-thin slices cured wagyu bresaola

serves 4

Baste the mushrooms with a little clarified butter and season with salt. Roast over a low fire, basting with extra clarified butter and turning when needed, until soft. Remove from the heat and cut into thumbnail-sized pieces.

Fold the mushroom pieces into the warm fermented grains and season to taste. Divide among bowls and cover each with three slices of the cured wagyu. Serve.

marron/fermented cucumber/pil pil

Like most of the food at IGNI, this is a combination of three relatively simple things brought together on the plate. The pil pil delivers an amazing, rich flavour but can be made with very little effort, the marron are a go-to ingredient for us as they react incredibly well to the fire, while the fermented cucumbers are something I always have around— they have a lovely lactic, salty-sweet balance, a nice crunch and pack enough flavour to stand on their own as a snack.

4 x 250 g (9 oz) marron
100 g (3½ oz) clarified butter

fermented cucumber

60 g (2 oz) rock salt
2 garlic cloves, sliced
½ bunch dill, roughly torn
10 baby cucumbers, washed

pil pil

1.5 kg (3 lb 5 oz) snapper bones, cleaned and dried
500 g (1 lb 2 oz) butter, diced
500 ml (17 fl oz/2 cups) fish stock
salt

serves 4

For the fermented cucumber, dissolve the rock salt in 2 litres (68 fl oz/8 cups) of water in a very clean bucket or container. Add another 6 litres (204 fl oz/24 cups) of water, stir well and leave to come to room temperature, then add the garlic, dill and cucumbers and cover with muslin. Leave to ferment at room temperature for 6–12 days.

For the marron, bring a large pot of water to the boil, place the marron in the water and leave for 10 seconds or until the shell begins to turn red. Remove from the pan and plunge straight into a bowl of iced water. Remove the head from the tail by twisting the two in opposite directions. Using scissors, cut along the underside of the tail, carefully peeling the shell away from the meat. Brush with the clarified butter.

Preheat the oven to 140°C (275°F/Gas 1). To make the pil pil, arrange the snapper bones on a tray with the butter and roast for 90 minutes. Pass the melted butter through a fine sieve, discarding the fish bones, and add to a heavy-based saucepan together with an equal amount of fish stock. Cook for 15–20 minutes over a low heat until the mixture emulsifies, then pass through a fine sieve and season with salt. Keep warm.

Place the marron onto a grill over a fruit wood fire and gently roll around until the flesh starts to set. Remove from the heat and carve. Serve with the pil pil and cucumbers, sliced into quarters lengthways.

may

We desperately need to get new plates—by my last calculation we have chipped or broken roughly three thousand dollars worth since opening. It's a lot of money wasted and that doesn't even include water glasses, wine glasses and all the odds and ends used for all the different snacks and butters or the pitchers used tableside for broths and sauces. It's an expensive waste really, mostly avoided by taking a little extra care, but that's hard to teach and keep an eye on.

> New plates always come with renewed inspiration, a new dish will just appear as if it was laying in wait or somehow came with the plates, a bonus of purchase. I'm not sure how it happens, it just seems to.

The problem I'm having is finding any or enough suitable plates at a price we can afford. Bespoke potters are out of the question, just too expensive at the moment. There is very little surplus cash to go around; however, somehow we need to afford plates and I need the bonus inspiration that comes with them. Desperately.

I've been putting off buying bowls I've found in a store selling mass-produced plates from Japan. They are decent enough that I can live with them and use them as a placeholder until maybe, hopefully, we can afford to spend some money on customised service pieces. It's not easy making all this work, the juggle of a new restaurant, the needs and wants.

So shitty black bowls it is, for now. I hate them already but the food looks better plated on them, a temporary relief from the stark white of our ordinary plates.

11 pm

I've been standing in the cool room as I like to do (I didn't even realise I did until Drew pointed it out one day). Here I am staring at all the bones and flesh hanging quietly, aging, in various stages of readiness, contemplating exactly what to do with it all. There are a few working parts of new dishes floating around, stages of thoughts and ideas, bits and pieces all without a home, waiting for that lightbulb moment when they make sense. Nothing's exact or even considered, new dishes often come by accident or a spontaneous moment of clarity. And then all of a sudden it dawns on me, I know exactly what I'll do with the honey vinegar I made two months ago for no apparent reason other than that we had just had an excess of great honey gifted to us by a novice beekeeper. And with that wilting radicchio that turned up at some stage during the week that keeps getting shuffled from one crate to the next. Standing there in the cool room after service, miraculously as if out of thin air, a new dish has arrived.

aged lamb rump/raw honey vinegar/radicchio and parsnip

We are only eleven days into the month but it feels like it's going on forever, maybe it's because I'm counting down the days to a break. Some days I don't really want to be here, the days I find it nearly impossible for reasons I'm not entirely sure of or willing to admit to myself. Sometimes I think if I stop now I could walk away, deal with the debt and convince myself I tried and that it just wasn't meant to be.

There's something about the space between these four walls that I can't settle into. I mean, there are moments that I love it, proud that we even got the doors open and finding myself believing in what we are doing 110 per cent, even letting myself indulge in the idea that I'm back doing what I'm supposed to be doing. But the other argument, that this is all I know how to do, so I have no choice but to do it, always raises its head. After all, what's the alternative? To wander around from one dead-end job to another? I can't let myself believe that's the path I should take, so here I am demanding myself to try and make peace with it, which is not an easy task.

Today we had the last of our guest chefs, Matt Wilkinson from Pope Joan, come and cook with us. I've always admired Matt's approach to putting produce first and never compromising flavour for technique, a long-held belief of mine as well.

> A menu prepared on the morning of the lunch, with Matt at the wheel. It comes as such a relief, these guest chefs, a chance for me to be in the kitchen and learn. We asked Mac Forbes, friend and wine maker, to come along and be part of the day, to pour his wines from the Yarra Valley, share stories and have a laugh with the guests. It's a great day.

We decided to set a big communal table, a nice way to do these events and a way of breaking down the barriers between the restaurant and guests, something we try and do each day with every service. We want our guests to feel comfortable and in some way create an environment that makes them feel like they can sit back and be taken care of, so we can interact on a level not seen in most restaurants, relaxed and full of personality with no barriers between the restaurant kitchen and our guests.

Despite the success of the guest chef lunches, and after careful consideration, we have decided not to continue with them for now. While being a great avenue to learn, I have a strong feeling we need to focus in-house, to make sure we are fully formed as a team and as a young restaurant, before we do anything that distracts us from our goals. First things first though, what are our goals, exactly? Do we even have any other than to be the best restaurant down an alley in Geelong?

I've decided to try and stop stressing myself about how quiet it can be and how we are going to pay the bills. Tonight we only have nine people booked, and I want us to focus on making those people feel like they are the nine most important people in Geelong, expending all our energy and attention on creating a bespoke experience just for them. This isn't an easy task for me, given how used I am to spending every second questioning everything I think or do. Still, I'll try to focus on each day as a new day, a chance to reset and push forward in what we are doing. Each day we have new guests and a chance to start fresh, each service should bring the promise of the unknown and, as a cook, that should be exciting.

Some pheasants arrived with our ducks this week, a friend of a friend was trial-farming them and thought we would like a few. I've got them hanging to dry out: the skin behaves so much better over the fire once left to dry a little. It's quite a nice thing to watch the meat and birds hanging and aging, slowly decaying to exactly the right point of deliciousness. I notice how yellow the skin has become, iridescent like an egg yolk. Actually, it would be quite nice to serve the roasted birds with a yolk sauce. I think I will try that tomorrow, slowly cooking the yolks in olive oil and blitzing them with fresh herbs until silky smooth. We have just finished drying some fermented greens; I'll taste them but I think if they have worked out they will have a nice acidity that could help cut the richness of the yolks. The simple joys of discovering a dish.

pheasant/yolk/fermented greens

What do I do with it? The fish, that is. Do I cure it? Smoke it? If I do smoke it, should I use a hot or cold smoke? Maybe there's a way to hang it somewhere high over the fire for the day and see what comes of it? Or perhaps I should cook it with lots of smoke quickly over hot burning wood.

I could just serve it raw? Thin slices quickly drenched in citrus and served with picked herbs and plants. Wait, no, I've seen that too many times before...

I could quickly cold brine it in a combination of acidic whey, salt and ice and see what that does to the texture. Or perhaps cook it slowly in olive oil until the whole side flakes apart, then serve it at room temperature with young garlic and those bitter leaves Bruce dropped off.

Today I quite enjoy this process of figuring out what to do, but there are times when I find it overwhelming and can become defeated by it all. Perhaps it's the pressure of trying too hard. I question my skills, my palate, pretty much everything I do, blocking any chance of getting anywhere. I know at times I'm my own worst enemy but I also know the way I work best—when it happens it happens, there's no use forcing it.

above: kohlrabi

aged lamb rump/raw honey vinegar/radicchio and parsnip

The honey vinegar here is a bit of an IGNI staple and is extremely versatile. We add it to dishes in place of sugar to bring sweetness or we use it, like here, as a way of cutting through fats. Try it spooned over chicken or drizzled over a fresh fruit salad. Put simply, if you like it use it—there are no rules.

1 x 200 g (7 oz) 42-day aged lamb rump, on the bone
1 radicchio head, leaves separated and white stems removed
80 g (2¾ oz) clarified butter
salt flakes

raw honey vinegar

300 g (10½ oz) raw honey
80 g (2¾ oz) raw apple-cider vinegar
2 lemon thyme sprigs
1 teaspoon mushroom soy
1 teaspoon mirin
pinch of salt flakes

parsnip purée

splash of olive oil
300 g (10½ oz) parsnips, cut into thumb-sized pieces
500 ml (17 fl oz/2 cups) milk
50 g (1¾ oz) cold unsalted butter
salt

serves 2

For the raw honey vinegar, gently warm all the ingredients in a heavy-based saucepan until combined (you want to be careful not to overheat this as you will kill off the honey's flavours). Set aside in a warm place for 4 hours. Pass through a fine sieve to remove any solids and set aside.

For the parsnip purée, heat the olive oil in a large heavy-based saucepan. Add the parsnip, milk and 500 ml (17 fl oz/2 cups) water, bring to a simmer and cook until the parsnips are soft and starting to fall apart. Strain, reserving the liquid, and leave to cool for 10 minutes, then transfer to a blender and blitz on high, adding the reserved cooking liquid slowly, to form a wet purée. Add the butter and season to taste.

Place the lamb rump fat-side down on a grill over a bed of embers and cook, turning every couple of minutes, for 30 minutes or until the fat has rendered. Transfer the rump to a grill over a hot flame and roast for 8 minutes. Remove from the heat and set aside to rest.

Brush the radicchio leaves with clarified butter and grill over a high heat until wilted and charring around the edges. Season with salt.

To serve, de-bone the lamb and divide it between plates together with the radicchio and parsnip purée. Drizzle over the honey vinegar to finish.

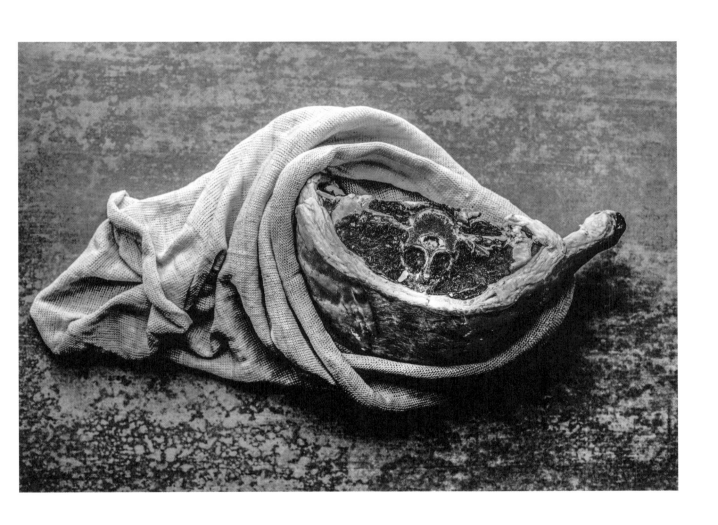

freshly churned butter/cultured butter

We make all our butter at the restaurant, sourcing our cream from the Schulz organic farm in Timboon, south-west Victoria. We start the cultured butter off at the end of the week and leave it to sit in a warm spot high above the fire's embers until we are ready to make it on the Wednesday morning.

Though butter-making might seem like a fiddly process, it's actually simple enough to have you wishing you tried it years ago. A lot of recipes will suggest washing the butter with lots of fresh water after straining it, but I prefer to let whatever buttermilk there is still on the butter remain at this point as I quite like its acidic flavour.

cold jersey cream
yoghurt or starter culture (for cultured butter)

makes as much as you like

For freshly churned butter, place the cream into the bowl of a mixer with the whisk attachment added. Mix on a medium speed until the butterfat starts separating from the buttermilk (the colour will change from white to yellow as this happens). Continue to mix until the fats have completely separated, then pour into a fine sieve and strain off the buttermilk.

For cultured butter, warm the cream in a saucepan to blood temperature (you can test this with a thermometer, which will read 36°C, or by sticking your finger into it—you shouldn't feel a temperature difference). Remove from the heat and stir through the yoghurt or culture, cover with plastic wrap and leave to sit in a warm place overnight, then refrigerate until cold before proceeding as you would for regular butter.

old ewe/new ewe

This favourite at Loam made its way over to the IGNI menu unchanged and is one of the very few things we make that has a formal recipe. It first made an appearance at Loam when my friend Olivia Sutton, of the cheesemonger Harper & Blohm, headed down for lunch. I knew Carles roquefort (which at that time was being impounded in Australia due to fears over listeria and was quite difficult to get hold of) was her favourite cheese, so I thought she'd enjoy trying it served like this. She was still talking about it years later, so when she was booked in for IGNI I put it back on the menu for her.

200 g (7 oz) sheep's milk yoghurt
25 g (1 oz) brown sugar
80 g (2¾ oz) Carles roquefort, chilled
12 mint leaves, very finely sliced

serves 4

Add the yoghurt and sugar to a large bowl and whisk to combine. Continue to whisk until the yoghurt is smooth and runny, then transfer to the freezer and leave to freeze overnight.

The next day, use a fork to scrape the frozen yoghurt into a snow-like texture. Return to the freezer until needed.

To serve, place a tablespoon of roquefort into the centre of four individual shallow serving bowls, cover with the frozen yoghurt 'snow' and scatter over the sliced mint leaves to finish.

potato and mussel sauce

This sauce is delicious and seriously easy to make. It's lovely and light and loaded with flavour and a naturally starchy texture that surprises a lot of people, who assume we must have used thickeners to make it. We use it with fish and shellfish, or with grilled vegetables like artichokes.

400 g (14 oz) king edward potatoes
400 ml (13½ fl oz) mussel stock
400 ml (13½ fl oz) chicken stock

makes 400 ml (13½ fl oz)

Cut the potatoes into thumb-sized pieces and add to a saucepan together with the mussel and chicken stocks. Bring to the boil and cook until the potatoes are overcooked and breaking up. Remove from the heat and leave to cool for 20 minutes, then transfer to a blender and blitz on medium to a smooth runny purée. Pass through a strainer to finish.

june

Three weeks, eighteen services until we close for a winter break. We need it. Everyone is a little shell-shocked—well, I am at least. I'm tired like I've never been before. Exhausted.

I've decided to go camping, something I've always wanted to do but have kept putting off, the excuse being there's never enough time and there is always work to be done.

I've booked a cabin in the basin of the Otways, deep in the forest with no phone service, internet or distractions.

I'm trying to forget the last six months.

Not in a bad way, not at all, rather, I'm trying to reset myself, to take a moment and reflect on the last three months and the opening of the restaurant. I've never taken time before, scared that if I stop I'll lose momentum moving forward.

> IGNI opened in what seems like a flash of moments, a series of reactions rather than a planned, cohesive attack. We didn't understand the space—how could we, there was very little time to get to know it—and we were under the heavy weight of expectation. Even if it was our own it was still ever-present.

For a brief time in our planning stages, IGNI was going to be a casual place, more of a bar than a serious restaurant, a place with no name, just a flashing neon sign saying open or closed. Loud music and bar food, something I could do easily—take a wage, work with great people and not think too deeply. 'Slingin' booze and slicin' ham', I'd joke.

However, the more we talked, discussed, begged and borrowed, it became apparent we weren't finished with the path we had started on years earlier at Loam. What was it that we missed, what was it that we wanted? Did we even know?

I argued to just build the thing and let the space tell us what it could become.

One thing Drew, Jo and I knew is that we wanted to create an experience, something people would engage with and something we all longed for in everyday life, something tangible we all felt was missing in a world of television chefs and Instagram posts.

From the moment we opened we felt like we were behind, finding seconds and minutes in each day to catch our breath and try to keep up. No one really talks about that time at the beginning of a restaurant. Those first few weeks and months are hard. In fact, one of the hardest things you'll do owning a restaurant is getting those doors open.

And it never really gets any easier, either—the self-doubt, the conflicting emotions, the panic of not being good enough. Holding your breath and hoping what you are doing is ok, or more than ok.

I ask myself time and time again why on earth I do it to myself.

Building a solid base for the fire is the most important part. A dry, stable base will help create an even bed of coals and embers. Fire is a mixture of fuel, heat and oxygen—these three elements are the life of a fire.

Start with dry tinder, anything you can find that isn't wet and will easily ignite. Leaves and small twigs work perfectly. The next step is to find some kindling, slightly larger twigs and branches, and to form a teepee over the tinder, before adding to the teepee with logs of chopped dry wood—these are best gathered from newly fallen or dead dried branches.

Another way of getting a good base for the fire is to build a Jenga-like structure over the tinder, allowing oxygen through for the fire to breathe. Once the fire has taken hold, slowly feed it with more medium-sized branches, gradually building up to firewood, logs and stumps.

I contemplate the day over a roughly made cup of camp coffee. I've never managed to master it. I take a walk to begin the day and start a little bit of early prep for tonight's dinner.

I have some old carrots that I dug out of the bottom of a tote in the cool room before we closed for the break. I prefer them this way, the flavours seem more at ease with one another—not pretty to look at but delicious, with concentrated sweetness.

I think about cooking them slowly over the embers of last night's fire, leaving them for hours to cook slowly and basting them when I remember with a little fat from the drippings I saved from last night's grill. They will need little attention throughout the day and will probably overcook, turn black and fall apart, but mashed with a little lemon and fresh cheese on grilled bread they will make a great afternoon snack with a cold beer.

While the embers are low I put a pumpkin on to cook in the ashes, poking holes in the skin to ensure it won't explode. I still don't care for it but Brecon, my mate I've convinced to tag along, loves it, so I'll shovel some glowing embers over it throughout the day and leave it to roast for as long as it needs, then forget about it until the afternoon. If it cooks in time I'll use it for tonight's dinner; if not, tomorrow's lunch.

As the fire starts to build the need for warmth grows and I add more wood. I have cabbages, which I'll cut deep gashes into and roast whole until black and tender—shredded, they will make a great base for a warm salad. Perhaps I'll wrap some potatoes in wet paperbark with butter and herbs, slowly baking them on the outside of the fire. They can take as long as they need—there is no hurry, no service, no seconds that will make the difference between success and failure. Time is on my side.

I've brought some live scallops from the bay with me that I'll clean and roast directly on the embers for a quick snack, perhaps with a splash of olive oil and horseradish, still raw but warmed by the fire.

I remember reading a quote some time ago by someone I can't remember, in a book long forgotten, but it went something like this: 'there is no better way to cook a chicken than over fire'. Or maybe it was on a menu... Either way, it's the truth. A well-raised chicken simply roasted over the fire cannot be beaten. So tonight I'm going to do exactly that, rubbing one with a little lemon, oregano and salt and leaving it to cook over the coals.

> It's nice to be here cooking for no reason, for no one in particular, and with no importance placed on time. Just cooking—simple, unrefined.
>
> Perhaps subconsciously that's why I chose fire at IGNI. I'm not sure I can claim the forethought because I don't recall it being a conscious decision, I just wanted something different from what I'd done before, something I didn't fully understand.

Maybe in some strange way it was to remind myself that I did love cooking, at some point. For the better part of a decade it consumed me. Perhaps it was to remind me I still do, if I just get back to the very basics of it all.

It's cold out and drizzling rain, colder than I remember it being this time of year, or maybe I'm just getting older. There is an ominous swirl of back and grey that blankets the sky and I'm anxious for a moment until I realise I have nowhere to be but right here, waking as the sun rises.

It's one of those moments that you kind of neglect in life, the simple moments I've had to teach myself to enjoy and even learn they exist; I've spent too much time just driving myself into the ground to succeed only to end up back at square one.

But the perfection we seek can be found in the simplest of things— radishes picked and eaten that very moment, or peas still warm from the sun and grown in soil that is alive. Idealistic, I know, but why is it we do what we do, what draws me and people like me to cooking, when we are constantly frustrated with the quality of produce we have available to us? Our milk is watered down and sold for next to nothing, supermarkets demand unachievable production costs of our farmers, our cheese is pasteurised, our vegetables are sprayed within an inch of their short shelf lives and have travelled further across our country than some people will do in a lifetime only to arrive in the supermarkets wrapped, wilting and in various stages of rot, placed on display with illuminating claims of being 'ready to cook'.

So why do I bother? I don't have an answer for that yet.

Cooking out here is different though, with just a fire for warmth and nourishment. No one cares if something is a little burnt or dry, in fact it's almost expected. I can't get away with that in a restaurant so cooking here has a certain freedom. It's a time with no distractions, no expectations and no eyes watching.

> I'm reminded today that three years ago I shut Loam. That day that seems a lifetime ago, like a day in someone else's life, so far removed from where I am now, sitting in a forest with the photographer Julian Kingma, contemplating writing and shooting this book. How do I respond to this memory? Was it me who closed Loam? Was it me who wandered lost in Tennessee for two years? And is it me now, opening IGNI? I don't feel like the same person, but people keep reminding me that I am. I feel I'm watching my life from a distance, watching it unfold from above.

I have a few photos of the last service we did. They seem so strange to look at, and I really don't recognise the person standing there leaning against a broken oven, long hair and no beard, sunken, skin and bones. He looks alien, eyes barely open from exhaustion, nothing more than a coloured shadow dressed in a chef's jacket and apron.

It's then that I realise that perhaps this is why I chose not to wear a chef's jacket at IGNI—the very thought of being, or even resembling, a chef was something I hated, something I'm still not comfortable with. Or perhaps it was the fact I was convinced I didn't want to cook anymore.

Either way, the thought of dressing in chef's whites made me feel like an intruder this time around.

G2220FF0011   G2220FF0011

quickly roasted scallops

I'm not a big fan of cooked scallops—I've always preferred eating them raw (and still serve them like this as a snack in the restaurant) but this relies on getting them live and fresh and using them immediately.

The scallops I took on this camping trip weren't quite as fresh as I had originally hoped, so I tried something different and cooked them like this. It gave them an intense, roasted shellfish flavour as well as a lovely, earthy smokiness and is something I've since taken back to the restaurant, where we cook them to order in the hot embers of the fire.

4 scallops in their shells, scallop meat trimmed and rinsed
80 ml (2½ fl oz) olive oil
pinch of salt flakes
1 fresh horseradish root

serves 4

Detach the roes from the scallop meat and roughly chop, adding olive oil and salt to form a rough paste. Spoon the paste over the scallop meat, grate over the horseradish and tie the shells together with string.

Place the tied scallops onto hot coals and leave to cook until you see the filling mixture start to bubble out of the side of the shells. Remove from the heat and eat immediately.

warm charred cabbage salad

If this is left in the right place in the fire it will slowly cook itself, needing little to no attention. Try adding leftover herbs or smoked fish to the salad before serving.

1 savoy cabbage
100 ml (3½ fl oz) olive oil
salt flakes

dressing

6 anchovies, minced
1 small garlic clove, minced
1 tablespoon green peppercorn mustard
juice of 1 lemon
1 egg
grapeseed oil
salt flakes and cracked pepper

serves 6–8

For the dressing, mix the anchovies and garlic together to form a paste, then add the mustard, lemon juice and egg and mix well. Whisk in enough grapeseed oil to bring everything together, then season with salt and cracked pepper.

Using a large knife, make a series of large incisions on all sides of the cabbage. Rub the cabbage with the olive oil and salt, then set it over the centre of a medium fire, or directly in the middle of the embers if you prefer. Roast until the cabbage is cooked through, testing it with a skewer to check if it is tender and moving it around the fire while cooking if the embers are intense.

Remove the cabbage from the heat and peel off and discard any burnt outer layers. Roughly chop the remainder and toss together with the dressing. Serve.

suckling pig belly/slow-roasted carrot

When I cooked this while we were camping I hung the suckling pig belly up over the fire to roast slowly, using the ambient heat of the fire and not paying it too much attention, though at IGNI we cook it directly over the fire. If set at the right height over a bed of embers, the carrots here will slowly steam in their own skins and turn a lovely black without overcooking. We've now taken this slow-cooking method even further in the restaurant, roasting the carrots on the grill over the fire for a day and a half and adjusting the height off the embers to bring out as much of their natural sweetness as possible.

suckling pig belly

> 1 kg (2 lb 3 oz) suckling pig belly
> 100 ml (3½ fl oz) grapeseed oil
> pinch of salt flakes

slow-roasted carrot

> 10 carrots
> 250 g (9 oz) butter, 200 g (7 oz) melted
>   and 50 g (1¾ oz) cold
> 200 ml (7 fl oz) chicken stock
> salt

serves 4–6

For the slow-roasted carrot, place the carrots over a bed of red gum embers and baste with the melted butter. Leave to cook, turning and basting every 10–15 minutes and tending to the fire as needed, for 3 hours, or until the carrots have turned soft and black.

Meanwhile, rub the pig belly with the grapeseed oil and salt and leave to sit at room temperature for 1 hour, then wipe off any excess oil and salt with a damp cloth.

Heat a splash of grapeseed oil in a cast-iron pan, add the belly skin-side down and, as it begins to sizzle, press down firmly with your hands. Continue to cook, applying a good amount of pressure and moving the belly around the pan, until the skin is golden. Remove the pan from the heat and turn the belly over to rest and finish cooking through.

To finish the carrots, warm the chicken stock in a pan. Add the carrots to a blender and blitz on high, gradually adding the chicken stock and cold butter until smooth. Season with salt and pass through a fine sieve.

Plate as you wish.

july

It's our first shift back after the winter break. The mornings are cold, the fire in the kitchen offering nice relief. We only have seventeen guests booked tonight for dinner and that's not enough to make a thirty-seat restaurant viable, which leads to the question always lingering in the back of my mind: what happens if this doesn't work?

On the upside, winter's vegetables are now at a somewhat decent price, and the jerusalem artichokes Bruce has been growing for us are ready. For the first time since we opened I have a plan ready and waiting for them: we are going to wrap them in foil and bury them in the coals from the fire overnight, roughly six hours, slowly steaming and dehydrating them just a little to concentrate the sugars, rendering them slightly chewy. We will serve them warm with a king edward potato and mussel sauce with horseradish and thin slices of cured wagyu. It dawns on me that it's basically meat and two veg—an Australian classic.

While we were away I had considered scratching all the dishes we were running before the break and starting fresh once we returned, using the new ideas that come after time away from the kitchen, but instead I've decided to keep the dishes the same and focus on refinement. Refinement of technique, flavour, plating. Keeping the dishes the same but making them purer, maybe even simpler, and the best versions of themselves. But perhaps it's just an excuse to minimise the pressure on myself to be always changing things, and maybe even a reason not to spend as much time in the kitchen as I have before.

> I still don't feel comfortable in this kitchen, or here at IGNI in general. It's a strange feeling. And I'm not even sure I understand the fire quite yet, this burning pit in the middle of it all that needs attention day in and day out, always reminding me it's there warming my back as I call service from the pass. It's been three years since I've had to cook for people in a restaurant, people with expectations. Three years since I've had to be en place and ready for service, three years since I've had to cook food that people will study, debate, discover, photograph and write about. Three years since I said 'Fuck it, I'm done', and walked away.

Is it this, the uncomfortable relationship I have with the fire and cooking, that is restricting us? The ugly truth is that it probably is—I just don't understand it and I'm fumbling through trying to find my way.

Am I slowing our development because of how unsure I am?

Is it all just mental? I'm finding it exhausting in a way I haven't experienced before. It wasn't always like this. I'm struggling to be in the kitchen at all, to be as creative and fluid as I once was. I get easily distracted, perhaps even a little scared, or, let's be honest, terrified. It's an odd feeling, being back in the kitchen. It still brings back bad memories. I've tried to snap out of it, this hole I seem to be in, but something just keeps chipping away at me, a voice inside my head on repeat telling me, 'You're not good enough; why are you doing this?' Perhaps it's right, maybe I'm not.

It's so draining, this constant argument with myself, so defeating, especially when I remember how much I used to love this.

I can't sleep. I'm not much of a sleeper anyway; seems it's the hours between service ending and the sun coming up that my head does most of its thinking. I can't help but think about how much is on the line, what all the people at IGNI have invested, the money spent and how much of this relies on me having my shit together. Fuck I hope it works out.

I scribble down a note to remind me to change the bread; we need a better version. I've thought about adding Point Henry saltbush to the rye for some time. I'll talk to the baker, Ben, to see if he wants to give it a go and see if it works.

The first weeks back are always the hardest. It's amazing how quickly your body stops being able to cope with fifteen-hour work days. My back aches, my feet are sore and there is a curious new pain in my left knee, one I haven't felt before.

I've lived and worked with constant pain from an old injury: my legs were pieced back together eighteen years ago with four steel rods to hold my hips in place. They hurt; sometimes I can't really walk, other times sitting is worse and there are some mornings I can't quite get myself out of bed, every move sending a thousand needles running up and down my nerves. I've never let it restrict me, never let it hold me back from the kitchen, preferring to just limp through and get the job done no matter how much pain I'm in. These days codeine helps. Stubborn? Maybe, but what's the alternative? Now it's a little harder to convince my body to agree; maybe it's a lack of will, but here I am doubled over a stainless steel bench wrestling marron into submission and wishing I was back in bed.

The mornings have felt colder than usual this winter and it's hard to get myself out of bed. The internal negotiations start when the first alarm goes off around 6 am. I spend the next thirty minutes contemplating a hot cup of coffee and a warm shower. The argument continues until I concede and get up with my second alarm, feeling like I've had no sleep at all.

Then there's the running around that is required to get the restaurant in order before I go in and start the never-ending list of prep for the day—the nitrogen to pick up, wild leaves and flowers to pick, organic flour, oils and seeds to organise from the health food store, dried fish, vinegars and greens to pick up and sort through at the Asian market. Then there are the phone calls to farmers and suppliers, emails and all the issues from the previous day to pay attention to, and, last but not least, there's last night's service to consider—what went right and, more importantly, what went wrong, What is it that needs refining, what needs immediate attention? Was the service actually any good?

Questions are bounced around from scribbled notes left in my book after a long service, notes from the day. Were we attentive enough? Was the timing of the kitchen ok? Were we efficient and productive? What dishes did I like and which need cutting? It's a never-ending cycle and, when you think about it, it's absurd, all this constant internal debate.

It's another quiet week for bookings. The two before the break were slow, with last-minute cancellations seeming to increase during the month, for reasons I'm not sure of. It's definitely concerning but I'm trying not to think about it too much, or let on that I am concerned. Still, it makes me wonder, are we doing a good enough job?

In all honesty I had hoped we would be busier by now, six months in and with positive reviews, but we aren't, really, and now I'm convinced we never will be. It's always a gamble opening a restaurant, especially one with thirty seats in the back alleys of Geelong, a fact I'm reminded of by nearly everyone who comes through the doors.

There's the constant surprise of the location, the alleyway: 'Why Geelong?' The doubts that we will actually survive, always with the lead in of 'we used to go to Loam', each question and concern placated with a repetitive, almost scripted response: 'The location has beautiful light that we fell in love with, the alleyway has charm, why not an alleyway?' (Read: it's all we could afford, we have had no money, and you're right, we might not survive.) Why Geelong? It has a beach, and again we have no money to afford city rents. Perhaps I'm just trying to convince myself that opening IGNI was a good idea.

> Now that we are settled back into kitchen life from a quick break I've decided I need to discover what the essence of IGNI is or might be. People ask, 'What is IGNI all about?' and it's a question I'm not really sure how to answer—it's just a restaurant, is it supposed to be something other than that? It's something I didn't really think about, something I never asked myself. Should I have?

I suppose, if I think about it, it's an effort to explore what we are doing, why we even do it; it's about trying to understand who we are and what we do, day in, day out in this black box in an alleyway in an almost forgotten industrial city not known for much outside of a football team.

I had thought, after returning from break, that I should start over with all the dishes and then changed my mind. I feel like I can't get settled, can't stand still and focus. And so I've changed my mind again. I'm going to try to start afresh as best as I can. I need to feel challenged, and feel like I'm not cheating, even if I'm the only one who would call it that. Dishes, flavours, combinations—anything I've had success with before— gone. I don't want to resort to old dishes I know people enjoyed at Loam. Things like old ewe new ewe, a course of sheep's milk blue cheese, frozen fresh ewe's milk and mint, three ingredients I know work and a dish I know people love; it's my get-out-of-jail-free card. I've dug into my bag of tricks a few too many times since opening and I get disappointed in myself for doing so, but it was either that or have nothing to offer, so I'll try this new strategy to see if I can kickstart some creativity.

I know this will make it harder, on myself and on the kitchen, maybe even harder than it has to be. Even so, I feel we need this, I need this, to make this deal with myself in the pursuit of moving even further away from what I have done previously as a cook. What that means, exactly, what it might mean for the restaurant, I'm not quite sure yet. I guess time will tell.

This focus might slow down the progress of the kitchen, but that's ok. Maybe it's even the right time to slow down a little—I've always gone at a thousand miles an hour. I know the boys in the kitchen are keen to learn and push, it's more for self-preservation I guess. I've witnessed it all go up in flames before, perhaps I'm afraid of it happening again.

Maybe this is me protecting everyone here, steadying the ship and keeping it pointed at the horizon, slowly on course. Perhaps it's just an excuse for losing my nerve creatively. I know I don't trust my instinct anymore, and it's all I know about cooking—it's the most important part, it's how I've cooked my whole career. I'm not one for more than a basic recipe; I can't seem to follow them most of the time. I struggle to understand them or get lost and confused in the method. I've tried to learn but I've never been able to master it. I much prefer to amble along, adjusting and adding when needed.

I just keep telling myself if it all goes up in flames I can blame it on the questionable location, and not my lack of nerve. I'm feeling the pressure in a way I've never felt before, new dishes and flavours used to come so easy, they would appear with the faintest of recognition, the smell of wood burning or the feel of a piece of meat, the sounds and smell of a farm we would be visiting. The grass, the trees, the ocean spray have all contributed to dishes or inspiration in the past. Ideas would bounce around in my head like a pinball machine, now they seem to come very rarely. I feel uninspired by almost everything, detached from what it was that once made me a cook.

And if I'm being honest it makes me a little scared and worried, because there is still a real concern that IGNI may not work.

1 am

I'm wide awake with a sense of dread that tomorrow is looming, that we will open for guests, and that in just a few hours I'll be back in the kitchen with the pressure of coming up with new dishes. It feels like it was forever ago that I had an idea worth exploring. I feel like I have nothing to give, no real ideas, no inspiration, just a faint willingness to keep doing this, to keep cooking.

I feel so confused about IGNI. I'd hoped the break would have given me time to feel comfortable with being in a kitchen again, but I'm here with a blank page—no notes, thoughts or even a plan for tomorrow.

16·07·2016

Finally it feels like we had a good service tonight. The timing from the kitchen was good, perhaps even a little too fast, and I'm pushing the front-of-house team to work quicker and in a more economical style to make the timing of service a little better—to understand that seconds in a service can be the difference between a good night and a complete disaster. I've seen it before, a kitchen in full collapse during service, the chaos and panic, the yelling and the tears, a dining room in complete meltdown. I've watched in terror as the realisation dawns that there is no way back from the shitstorm around you.

In a kitchen you learn that every step counts. In fact, I used to count my steps in between the oven and the pass, reducing them where I could to make me more efficient during the day. Every action needs to be as tight as possible and you need to be always prepped, always paying attention, working fast and then faster the next day because at any second another task will be thrown onto that already impossible workload and you'd better be ready or god help you if you're not.

I want the front-of-house to be more like that. I know they can't be, completely, of course. They can't end up like chefs—bitter, twisted and a little fried from the heat and stress. They are supposed to be the pleasant ones, the saviours, after all. The guys we have out the front are good, actually really good; they all work so well together and with me, and they are in it for IGNI to succeed. I just need to convince them all to let go a little and to relax, to take a breath and let their personalities take over. I know if they can just do that all the other details that I harp on about will fall into place. Perhaps I should take my own advice.

I also wish they would stop breaking glasses. They're expensive.

I've been ignoring my phone for the last thirty minutes, trying to write this book, but it's been beeping at me all day and I'm tired of it. Reaching over to turn it off I see a text that reads, 'Congratulations on your nomination, so well deserved.'

What the hell does that mean? Being nominated for any awards was so far out of my mind I have no idea what it could be referring to. Up until right now I was convinced we had fucked it all up.

The message reveals that we have been nominated for a national restaurant award, Best New Restaurant, in *Gourmet Traveller* magazine. Holy shit, how did that happen? How were we even considered? I mean, there's some big guns listed and we have only been open for seven months.

I stop for a minute to consider how amazing this is for our restaurant, what this could mean or does mean. I guess it's a validation of sorts, and after a long sigh I feel the weight I have been carrying lifted. A sigh of relief, a moment of satisfaction, a comforting and sobering thought.

I'm going to need a minute to digest this.

I see the word IGNI out of the corner of my eye—it's popped out at me from the magazine that's open on the kitchen bar. I stop to read it and see that we have been nominated for not one award, as I thought, but two. IGNI has been nominated for Best New Restaurant and Regional Restaurant of the Year. I'm amazed and a little taken aback. We are in great company; Hubert in Sydney and Heston Blumenthal's Melbourne outpost of Dinner are up for Best New, and in the Regional Restaurant of the Year category I see we are with Brae and—I know what's coming before I turn the page, I know what'll be there and nothing I can say, pray or hope for will change it—the other restaurant nominated is owned by the very people that caused me to fall out of love with cooking and lose everything. It's unimaginable.

I guess this is the shit that glossy television shows don't show you. Nowhere is a signature required, you don't sign up for it, or I don't know, perhaps you do when you have a single focus, when everything you do is centred around achieving a single goal, a focus so intense and true you can't quite see straight, you learn to see nothing else; you can even forget the outside world exists. I truly never considered it, not once.

This should be a happy time, right? This should be a time for me to feel proud of my restaurant, of the team and of what we have achieved. A restaurant barely six months old has just been nominated for not one but two national awards in *Gourmet Traveller* magazine, and in the company of the best in the business. I'm in total shock and surprise, and I do feel proud, of myself and of my team, but defeated too, distracted and anxious about how this might turn out.

I get the weird feeling everyone is avoiding me and being overly nice. I'm just quietly going about my day, working on something I can't quite focus on—I'm too deep in thought to consider these small turnips I'm cleaning in the hopes of turning them into a snack for tonight. The last few years have been something of a bizarre, crazed, schizophrenic adventure, with moments of great loss and others of profound discovery. I realise that being nominated is a huge achievement, something we could have only hoped and dreamed of before we opened the doors in January.

I feel sad that perhaps the guys who have worked and continue to work so hard don't get to enjoy the moment because of the obvious, aware of the giant elephant in the room. Maybe they don't even care, perhaps it's just me walking on eggshells being careful not to wake the self-destructive beast inside.

I've smashed myself into a thousand pieces over the past two years because it's been easier than dealing with shit like this, but this time I refuse to head down that same path. I will stand and be stronger.

27·07·2016

Dear Jodi and Greg,

I want to thank you for today, for letting our small team intrude into your little piece of paradise, the farm.

I remember when I first met you, Greg was fresh from an abattoir, the death run no small farmer enjoys. You pulled up to Loam tired from an early day with ducks to sell, a buyer had fallen through. I bought all you had and hung them in the cool room to age a little over the Christmas break. I came back some ten days later to find the power had gone out not long after closing and we had lost all of the ducks; maggots had intruded and all your hard work had gone to waste. It broke my heart.

Mostly I want to thank you for awakening something in me, something I thought I'd buried forever or lost beneath the scars of a few nasty years. What you do, your farm, your ducks, inspires me in a way I'd long forgotten. Today you made me resolve to do better.

From somewhere buried deep the visit to your farm reawakend that staunch belief I once so fiercely held that I can make a difference, that I can affect the world in my own small way. Well, at least my world, the one I choose to create and live in, with the way I treat people—staff and guests—the food we serve and the way I expect those around me to treat each other in our world, at IGNI.

What we do as cooks and restaurateurs starts with you and your lovingly raised ducks. My admiration for you, out on a limb as you are as a small farmer in Victoria, and for those others forging the same path, is unending, and I am very honoured to be in some small way a part of what you do.

Thank you.

Another quiet lunch today. The winter weather has well and truly settled in, the brown and orange hues of autumn conceding to the pewter grip of winter. It's wet and miserable, a time I used to love and find inspiring, the coastal plants so lush and green against the steel grey of the ocean, the smell of the wet air hanging in the cold mornings as I wandered through frosted grass picking for the day's menu. Today though it finds me longing for the warm summer's sun.

We've had a group of five just cancel for lunch so now we are left with just three groups of two. It's deathly quiet, depressing. I knew these winter months would be hard, but this is quieter than I'd expected. My mind wanders again to the prospect of having to close, to just shut the doors and walk away. The very thought makes me feel anxious and nauseous.

Our first two tables have been seated, both on five courses, but thankfully both deciding to go with the matching wine option.

It's just then that Jo appears in front of me, eyes wide, jutting her head in the direction of table four, which has just been seated. I don't really understand what she's trying to tell me until I glance up and see the head reviewer from the *Herald Sun*. I turn to let the kitchen know, my concerned look sending a nervous tension through the kitchen and front-of-house team.

I'm worried that the dining room feels too stark and sterile. We need to get some flowers, to get new life in here. It's too grey, too much concrete. I'll talk to Jo about it. Or maybe we need new artwork, or… I don't know, maybe I'm just grumpy, I shouldn't really be thinking about this right now anyway; my mind is wandering, perhaps in an effort to ignore the fact that we are about to be reviewed again. I still have no confidence in what I am doing.

Our reviewer is scanning the wine list, focused and intent, I'm convinced, on finding a spelling mistake or a creased page. I worry about these things, maybe because they feel out of my control. I check with the boys in the kitchen to make sure we are all en place, ready for action, 'Yes, Chef', comes at me, short and sharp, but I'm not convinced. I know the importance of this, or perhaps I'm not convinced that I'm ready for this. I know what a difference it can make for our little restaurant in the alley, for everybody who works here.

I feel the weight of this whole place, constantly, not just the food, not just the kitchen but every detail, from plates to lighting to how the bill is presented. There is no big picture here yet, just a collection of a million minute details we need to sort out.

We need this to go well. We need it to go better than well. I have confidence in the team to do that; it's me I'm worried about.

Dinner was a non-event, fully booked but odd, people just came and left with no real excitement. We usually have a great interaction with our guests but the room feels strange. I can't put my finger on it, something just feels off. It frustrates me that I can't tell what it is—it feels like a waiting room.

Service feels disjointed. There's no flow or rhythm and it is in no way refined, our timing seems to be so out of sync—six people doing their own thing all at different times. It's like watching bumper cars going around and around until they crash into one another. No one seems to notice—it was a night that felt like none of our diners wanted to even be there.

I keep asking the same questions. How was the night? Are diners sitting too long with pairings before the food arrives? Do people have empty plates for too long? Are we being attentive, are our guests being rushed somehow? Is the kitchen too fast? Too slow? Are we giving the guests an experience, something more than just dinner? I feel the urgency to get it figured out, we definitely should know this by now.

But maybe that's just how it goes. Service is made up of so many moveable parts and I've always been locked away before, hidden behind the walls of a closed kitchen under fluorescent lights. Now I'm out here in the open, on display, and so is my team. Everything they do is right in front of me and everything I do is right in front of them and everything we do is on show for our guests. I don't feel good about today; I feel like I'm on the verge of losing my shit out of the frustration of trying to make this all click.

For now I think I'll just go home and forget today happened. I'm in no mood to be here.

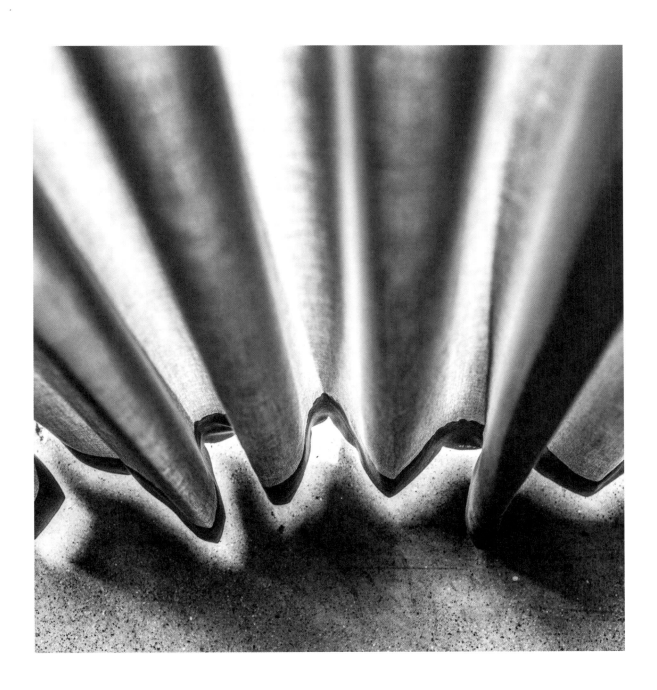

squid/chicken fat and marron broth

This dish was born from economic necessity. While I love to cook with marron, at $20 or so each they are expensive, so we need to get a second dish out of them. Thinking bisque-wise I started by experimenting with roasting the shell heads fiercely over the fire but the result was a little bit bitter, so we tried it again, starting the shells in an inch or so of chicken fat with some fennel tops and carrots, which lent the shells a nice sweetness and left us with this rich, earthy broth.

Some of the best squid and cuttlefish comes from Port Phillip Bay and when it's on I often order it in for the restaurant without a plan for what to do with it. Used raw here it provides the dish with a smooth textural element that is mirrored by the nice, silky mouthfeel of the broth.

1 x 500 g (1 lb 2 oz) squid
saltbush berries, to garnish

chicken fat and marron broth

6 marron heads and claws
100 g (3½ oz) roasted chicken fat
1 onion, sliced
3 carrots, roughly chopped
3 young fennel tops
3 litres (101 fl oz/12 cups) chicken stock
splash of mushroom soy
splash of mirin

serves 4

To prepare the squid, hold the squid body with one hand and the head in the other and pull in opposite directions. Clean the cavity and wash with running water, then remove the wings by sliding your fingers down the seam, removing the membrane as you go. Cut the squid tube in half lengthways, then stack the tube halves on top of each other, wrap tightly in plastic wrap and freeze overnight.

For the chicken fat and marron broth, roast the marron heads and claws over an open fire until red and aromatic.

Melt the chicken fat in a heavy-based saucepan, add the onion, carrot and fennel cook until softened. Add the roasted marron shells and sauté for 3 minutes, then pour over the chicken stock and simmer until reduced and golden red in colour. Season with mushroom soy and mirin to achieve a nice balance of sweet and savoury, then strain through a fine sieve. Set aside.

When ready to serve, remove the squid from the freezer and, while still frozen, slice into thin strands with a very sharp knife. Leave to defrost at room temperature then divide it between four deep serving bowls. Heat the broth, ladle it over the squid and garnish with saltbush berries to finish.

jerusalem artichokes cooked in coals overnight

I like to cook jerusalem artichokes like this, rather than puréeing them or making them into soup, as it keeps them whole and of themselves. Left in the embers overnight the artichokes almost cook from the inside-out—steaming in their own skins, reducing in size and concentrating the flavour.

1 kg (2 lb 3 oz) jerusalem artichokes
400 g (14 oz) king edward potatoes
salt flakes
fresh horseradish root, to serve
100 g (3½ oz) cured wagyu, cut into paper-thin slices

serves 8–10 as a side dish

Wash any dirt off the artichokes, then place on a wire rack in a heavy-based heatproof dish. Cover with foil and place on a bed of coals. Shovel more coals over the top of the artichokes and leave overnight, or for a minimum of 6 hours.

Chop the potatoes into thumbnail-sized pieces, add them to a pan together with 1 litre (34 fl oz/4 cups) water and bring to the boil. Boil until the potatoes begin to break apart, about 15 minutes. Strain, reserving the cooking liquid, and leave to cool to room temperature.

Once both the potatoes and the cooking liquid are cool, add the potatoes to a blender and blitz, adding the cooking liquid gradually to loosen as you go, to form a smooth sauce. Season with salt and keep warm.

To serve, pour a little of the potato sauce onto a warm serving plate and top with three of the artichokes. Grate over a little fresh horseradish and lay three pieces of the cured wagyu over the artichokes to finish.

august

Today was one of those days when all the stars aligned, creatively anyway. Three new dishes, three upbeat chefs and three confused front-of-house. I never tell them what's going on, so when new dishes happen they just appear between services or sometimes even in the middle. Secretly I think Drew likes it—the mystery, the smoke and mirrors—Jo, however, always has a much more concerned outlook because she is responsible for the pairing of the dish. I should get better at remembering that.

The jerusalem artichokes that we had been leaving under warm coals overnight have finally worked out. We had been trying for a few weeks to see what would happen, how they would react to being buried in embers and left to cook overnight in the remaining heat of the fire. It seemed a shame to be wasting that left-over energy.

It's taken some time to get them just right, not to burn them, or dehydrate them into shrivelled, misshapen balls. We figured if we raised them off the heat using a mishmash of trays, bricks, tin foil and cake racks and put a lid over the pit we could treat it more like an oven. The result was a texture somewhere between steamed, baked and roasted, the artichokes becoming like silk, something I had not experienced before. Plus it's a prep job that can happen overnight while we sleep—perfect.

The second dish that worked out for us today was a mandarin course, one of my favourite citrus to work with. I juiced them whole-skin, pips, pith, the works. I'd been a fan of this idea since tasting it done with oranges years ago while travelling through Spain. Then I turned this juice into a light sorbet, naturally sweet and bitter.

Friends of the restaurant who keep bees just near the botanical gardens had dropped by a jar of late spring honey, floral from the flowers of the gardens, and golden, much like the mandarins in colour. Immediately the two made sense together, even if it was just visually. But how was it to come together? It made sense to me but how was it to translate on the plate?

I'm a fan of honeycomb made using real honey, not just sugar, so I thought if I got the sugar and the glucose to the right temperature, just before adding the bicarbonate of soda, I could quickly whisk the honey through and keep the integrity of its flavour. The result was a honeycomb that tasted like the honey in the jar.

Tasting the two together made sense, but it needed an anchor of some sort, some other element to tie it all together—a sourness and something fatty. We had been playing with a cultured cream, something food cooked over the fire likes. It was fatty and acidic due to the bacteria used in the process, in fact it was perfect. A few frozen drops of soured cultured cream that in time would melt, releasing a fatty dressing of sorts. Sweet, sour, bitter—this made sense. We had a new dessert.

mandarin/cultured cream/honeycomb

The third dish was more of an extension of a dish we had on when we opened, potato noodles with society garlic, a simple dish relying on the flavours of onions and garlics from the garden. Those ingredients had long since finished for the season so I started to cook the potatoes in roasted chicken fat and garlic instead, adding pippis and raw egg yolk and treating it like a pasta. We had another dish.

king edward potatoes/goolwa pippies/egg yolk

I spent most of the morning trying to find a continuous source of inspiration in our new home. The winter skyline and household trees can only do so much on the walk to work. Our new urban environment is in complete contrast to where I was before. Until now inspiration had never been an issue for me, out there among the rugged landscape— the farm, the sea, the wild coast of southern Victoria, the old restaurant sitting on a farm somewhere down a long dust-laden, forgotten road. It's a different environment now, a whole different vibe: bitumen, red bricks and broken glass, complete with fire—a pit of flames burning at the heart of it all. It seems edgier, more abrupt. The change wasn't intentional, it just happened.

The morning light laminates the restaurant in grey and washed pinks, and it's a calming light. It sends my mind racing thinking of desserts, whipped pink lady apple ice cream, the ashes from the fire somehow incorporated into the dish just like the colours of the room. I think over the idea—perhaps apple slowly cooked in salted caramel with crisp milk and onion, something I quite like in a dessert—handled right it adds a sweet bitterness. The thought floats off and onto making a cup of coffee for the boys in the kitchen. I envy them, going about their day, cooking under careful instruction. It's not like the challenges I face, constantly racked with the guilt of having no new dishes, or not enough. It's particularly frustrating given the day before yesterday it seemed so easy. I have absolutely no idea how to change it. It's all mental, a loss of confidence, and I know that. We have actually had a pretty good run when I really think about it; sixty-four dishes have come and gone from the menu in seven months. I've been far from happy with most of them, but there has been at least sixty-four times we have created something. I have to try and remember how good it feels when we do that.

This weather, the cold, the grey, the constant drizzle, makes me miss the wild teal my friend Simon would bring to the old restaurant. It was this time of year he would head off with uncles, cousins and grandparents to shoot on the rice fields, a family tradition. After a weekend of camping and a long drive home he would drop his bounty off at the restaurant—his reward a cold beer. I would carefully remove any buckshot, let them hang for a week or two, cook them in a little brown butter and serve them to a few special guests. Simple and a pleasure to cook.

Simon doesn't shoot anymore, and I miss that.

Times have changed.

Messy service again tonight, and I'm starting to get angry and frustrated. This week is getting a little bit busier and we simply aren't doing a good enough job, nowhere near the level I expect us to be at, but it's hard to jump up and down, pointing fingers, when I don't feel like I'm at the level I need to be at either. I feel like we are running out of time to get this right, and I can feel the urgency in my chest. I have to say something: I have to create a panic so we change gear; it's now or never, this is it… wake up.

I'm also a little on edge. The *Gourmet Traveller* awards are next Wednesday. I know we won't win, there's no chance of it, but deep down I secretly really want to. Who wouldn't, for the validation, perhaps, or revenge, maybe? I know the rest of the staff can feel my tension—to be expected I guess—and it can be a good thing for everyone to feel as though they are on notice, including me. I want the win for them also, for all the hard work and faith they have put into IGNI. We can only cross our fingers and hope.

I'm nervous sitting here, I'll admit that. I really didn't expect to be nominated and a part of me doesn't want to be here. The whole night passes in a flash, a series of intense moments I just can't seem to keep up with.

There are a lot of lights on in here.
I'm coughing from the chilli.
I need a drink.
It's smokey in here.
What time is it?
I'm nervous/nauseous.
Hey there's Dan, 'Hey mate, how you been?'
God this cocktail is sweet, liquid palm sugar, I need a beer.
Wait, I promised myself I'd be an adult tonight.
But I'm nervous.
I need another drink.
There's a lot of green in this room.
There's Drew, where's Jo?
'Hey Pat, thanks for tonight, wow, I still can't believe we're nominated.'
What time is the flight in the morning?
I better not have another drink.
There's the man himself, David Thompson, in his new restaurant.
I wish I could cook like him.
What am I doing here?
That's my name on the table.
'Hey Neil, nice to see you. Sure I'll have a drink.'
Shit, that's one of our categories, Regional Restaurant of the Year.
Why are you handing me an award?
So many cameras.
IGNI won?
This champagne tastes nice.
Well, we didn't expect to win.
Wait, we won, holy shit.
Where did I put my drink?
Who am I hugging?
What time is it?
Jesus Christ, how many chillies are in this thing?
The food's so goddamn hot.
This taxi smells funny.
'Hi mate, good to see you, it's been a while.'
Is that octopus? I like this room, very decadent, nice one Hubert.
It's late.
Ahh the hotel, clean sheets.
Thank fucking god we won.
We did it.
I survived/we survived.
We won.

IGNI has been named Regional Restaurant of the Year in *Gourmet Traveller* magazine.

18·08·2016

This plane is taking forever to land; it just seems to be circling above the water. I'm ok with it; it's a moment to enjoy and reflect on the year up to now. What's next? How do we continue to grow and keep getting better, how do we get over the hurdles we are facing and live up to our new title? Where do we go from here?

19·08·2016

We have all safely landed from the high of winning the award and now it's back to reality. Crazy, when I think about it. I'm very proud of our little team.

Bruce, our dirt man, as he is now affectionately known since the review in *The Age*, brought in a bag of greens from a plant he was confused about. He claims, somewhat to his own surprise, to be trying to grow a yam of sorts, but instead he's ended up with what he describes as an 'odd looking parsley'. 'Beats me,' he says, chewing on a stalk, and 'tastes like dirt', before drifting off on a rant about a mixed bag of seeds he dropped in the hot house and now has no idea what's growing where. After some more consideration he guesses it could be hamburg parsley or hamburg rooted parsley; he remembers planting that somewhere. He shrugs his shoulders and heads off out the door and back to the farm.

I'm excited. I had long ago talked with Bruce about growing what I knew as parsley root, a discovery made while spending some time in Budapest years earlier. It is a fantastic root vegetable, not dissimilar to parsnip only with a strong parsley flavour. I'll need to send Bruce a text to remind him to dig up the roots for a sauce or purée. The leaves look and taste a lot like flat-leaf parsley, but there is a subtlety to them I can't quite put my finger on. The leaves are broad in texture and look like they will handle heat quite well.

Brushing the leaves and stems with clarified butter and charring them over the coals, just out of reach of the flame beneath, brings out the sweetness and adds a nice char to those leaves that yield to the fire and burn slightly.

I've been playing with a sauce of dried *shungiku* for the pigeon we have been aging. I'll use the whole plant—stalks, leaves and flowers—in addition to the leftover herbs from the previous week, mainly tarragon and marjoram, all mixed and blended with leek blackened in the coals. The sauce is a complex one, each flavour dominating with every taste, and the intricate sweetness of the hamburg parsley will, I think, give the balance the dish needs. I consider it, refining my thought process a little more. I've been nervous to change dishes on a whim like this, something I used to do all the time, but in a sudden kick of excited adrenaline I think fuck it, let's go with it. Mid-service I call Jo over and tell her we have a new dish.

It feels good.

aged squab/dried herbs/hamburg parsley

We had a couple in today, guests that were at both the first and last service we ever did at Loam, a lifetime ago. They have come to see us again, in the new place, to see how we have grown or if we have at all.

> It's a strange way to look at your life and career, through the eyes and appetites of others. I never really thought about it before, all the celebrations and special occasions we must have cooked and served.

For some it was a promotion, a birthday or anniversary, for others an engagement or just a night out away from the kids, a catch-up with old friends or an escape from the drudgery of the working week—a safe haven of sorts, a refuge for the working weary.

In some ways, it's a nice reminder of why we do this, what keeps us going.

I love this time of the year, the days warming from the winter, the light staying for a few minutes longer each day. The wild onion has started to flower, announcing that spring is here, although the weather isn't convincing me yet; it's still cold and grey.

I'm headed off to where I used to pick the wild onion years ago, more out of function than excitement. We have just run out of the onion flowers I pickled last year, long before opening IGNI. We have been serving them with a cheese I made around the same time. I'll pickle more this year if I can. I know I want to make something with all the leftover trimmings and flowers that don't make the cut for garnish. I always feel bad about throwing them away since the season is so short.

I've been thinking about a mussel and wild onion broth, or maybe a sauce. I've thought about it for quite some time, long before the season had started. I'll sauté a handful of mussels and wild onion stalks with pepper leaf—they grow side by side and just seem to make sense together. Then I'll let it simmer in fish stock for thirty minutes, strain and reduce it, before finishing it by whisking in a handful of cold cultured butter and freshly chopped chervil. A nice, lightly flavoured sauce for seafood.

I'll see if I can get it done in time for the weekend.

above: oyster plant

king edward potatoes/goolwa pippies/egg yolk

2 king edward potatoes, washed and peeled
salt
200 g (7 oz) goolwa pippies
100 g (3½ oz) roasted chicken fat
a splash of apple-cider vinegar, plus extra if necessary
4 egg yolks
12 bronze fennel fronds

leek ash

1 leek, ends removed
extra-virgin olive oil, to drizzle

serves 4

Cut the potatoes into long continuous noodles using a spiral cutter.

Wash the potatoes thoroughly in cold water until the water runs clear, then transfer to a saucepan of salted boiling water and blanch for 30 seconds. Drain the potato noodles and refresh in a bowl of ice-cold water.

For the leek ash, cut down the leek lengthways and separate the layers. Wash and dry, then drizzle with olive oil and season well, then place over a low fire and leave until blackened and completely dried out. Leave to cool, then transfer to a blender and blitz to a powder. Set aside.

Heat a heavy-based saucepan until hot, add the pippies and 100 ml (3½ fl oz) water, cover with a lid and cook for 4 minutes. Remove the pippies from the saucepan, take the meat from the shells and divide between four deep serving bowls.

Warm the chicken fat in a saucepan, add the potato noodles and cook until warmed through. Season with salt and add a splash or two of vinegar to taste, then pile over the pippies. Top each bowl with an egg yolk and finish with the fennel fronds and a few pinches of the leek ash.

broccoli heart/macadamia/cabbage oil

2 small broccoli heads
olive oil
salt flakes
yarrow flowers, to serve

cabbage oil

1 bunch cavolo nero (tuscan cabbage)
200 ml (7 fl oz) grapeseed oil

macadamia

50 g (1¾ oz) stale sourdough bread
1 garlic clove
120 g (4½ oz) macadamia nuts
50 ml (1¾ fl oz) extra-virgin olive oil
35 ml (1¼ fl oz) aged sherry vinegar
salt flakes and freshly ground black pepper

serves 4

To make the cabbage oil, blanch the cabbage leaves briefly in a saucepan of boiling water, then drain and refresh in ice-cold water to stop the cooking process. Pat dry, then transfer the leaves to a blender or food processor with the oil and blitz together for 3 minutes. Strain and transfer to the freezer to chill until needed.

For the macadamia, put the bread in a bowl, cover it with water and leave it to soak for 30 minutes. Once soaked, squeeze the excess water from the bread, then add it to a blender or food processor with all the remaining ingredients and 135 ml (4½ fl oz) water. Blitz together until combined, then season to taste. Pass through a fine strainer and set aside.

Remove the outer florets from the broccoli heads down to the very centre. Peel the thick outer layer from the broccoli cores, then cut them in half lengthways.

Bring a saucepan of salted water to the boil, add the broccoli halves and blanch for 10 seconds, then remove with a slotted spoon and refresh in ice-cold water. Repeat the process twice more, then pat the broccoli halves dry with paper towel, brush with olive oil and season with salt.

Place the broccoli halves cut-side down onto a grill set over a medium fire and leave for 6 minutes, or until a nice char has developed. Turn the broccoli halves over, remove from the heat and keep warm.

To serve, spoon the chilled macadamia sauce onto individual serving plates and top with the broccoli hearts. Drizzle over a little of the cabbage oil and garnish with yarrow flowers to finish.

mandarin/cultured cream/honeycomb

I love the flavour of citrus skin and sometimes I happily chew on it as it is. Juicing the mandarins whole with the seeds and skins—like they do in Spain—means the sorbet contains all those lovely essential oils which lend it the bitterness I love. Combined with the lactic tang of the cultured cream and the floral crunch of the honeycomb, this has become one of our most popular desserts.

500 g (1 lb 2 oz) mandarins, skin on
125 g (4½ oz) glucose
1 egg white
50 g (1¾ oz) freeze-dried mandarin

cultured cream

100 g (3½ oz) cultured cream
100 g (3½ oz) sour cream
2 litres (68 fl oz/8 cups) liquid nitrogen

honeycomb

415 g (14½ oz) caster (superfine) sugar
150 g (5½ oz) glucose
65 g (2¼ oz) honey
20 g (¾ oz) bicarbonate of soda (baking soda)

serves 8

Juice the whole mandarins, strain and let settle, then strain again. Weigh out 125 g (4½ oz) of the mandarin juice, add the glucose and mix together well. Churn in an ice cream machine, adding the beaten egg white halfway through the process, until frozen.

For the cultured cream, whisk together the cultured cream and sour cream and place the mix into a squeeze bottle. Drip the mix into a bowl filled with liquid nitrogen to form small balls. Repeat until all the mix is used, scoop the balls out of the liquid nitrogen and place immediately in the freezer. Discard the liquid nitrogen.

For the honeycomb, stir the sugar, glucose and honey together with 75 ml (2½ fl oz) water in a large heavy-based saucepan over a medium heat until dissolved. Bring to the boil and heat until the temperature of the sugar mix reaches 160°C (320°F). Remove from the heat and let settle for a second, then whisk in the bicarbonate of soda and pour into a lined tray. Leave to settle until cooled, then break into rough pieces

To serve, divide the cultured cream spheres, freeze-dried mandarin and honeycomb pieces among plates and top each with a scoop of mandarin sorbet.

september

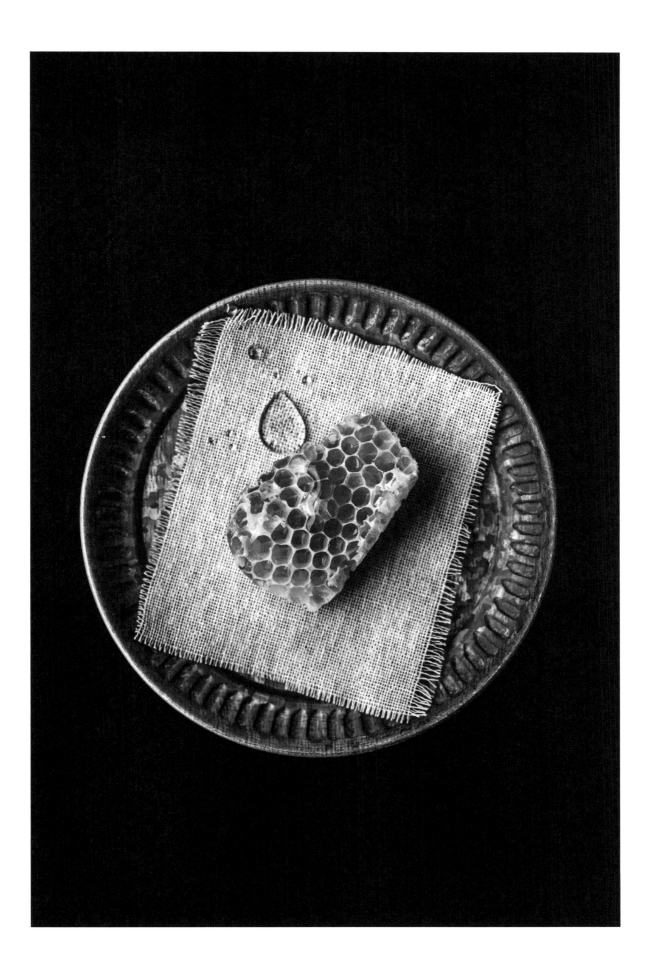

I keep thinking over and over, was IGNI a journey to finish what I started? Somewhere to figure it all out? Or was it just somewhere to send my cooking to die: IGNI the coffin, the big black box with a fire burning at the centre of it all, a cremation of everything that has come before.

Was the fire intended to ignite something? To cleanse the wounds and cauterise the lacerations left from the last few years? Or a place to rise triumphant from the ashes, as the media has alluded? I'm not sure. Maybe it's just circumstance, a result of stumbling around with nowhere to go, looking for a place to hide, somewhere to call home, something to do with my hands. Or is it simply that I just wanted to finish the job that I wasn't able to finish before, this time with the option to burn it all down—a place, a restaurant, a life firmly under my own control.

I could just be done with it, just walk away.

03·09·2016

It's still not that busy. Lunches are pretty much non-existent, ranging anywhere between two covers to maybe ten if we are lucky. It's a little awkward serving two people in a restaurant that just won a national award and it is quiet, deathly quiet in fact. The dinners are ok, however we have decided to drop to nine tables (from ten) in an effort to refine our service, refine the whole experience, really, not that that makes a difference for lunch at the moment. While the dinners are all right we really need the lunches to do well, especially since we also decided to close the extra day in an effort to sustain some sort of work–life balance. We are now doing six services in four days—Thursday to Sunday—so we need all the services to be full.

We are firmly on the radar, we have been validated, given the stamp of approval, so why are we still so quiet? Why am I still looking at twenty-six empty chairs? I can feel my mood has changed with the stress of each passing week. My body has started to break down on me. I'm tired all the time, my legs in constant pain, my body worn out and muscles twisted from holding on to all this nervous tension. It feels like we aren't getting anywhere, and in my head all of this feels pointless.

above: slippery jack mushrooms
opposite: zucchini flower

It's one of those moments when you see a picture of yourself but don't recognise it's you. I'm standing in line waiting for my morning coffee, staring at the front page of *The Age*, and there I am, front top corner. What am I doing on the cover of *The Age*?

I am in one of those awkward chef poses that photographers make you do, standing like an idiot with my arms up doing god knows what. For some reason I'm reluctant to open the paper and see what's inside. It's stupid really. I know it's not sinister, and I haven't done anything wrong—it's not like I'm wanted for armed robbery. It's for the restaurant, I know that, so why not just open it up and take a look? I will, straight after this coffee.

And there it is—holy shit, I've been nominated for Chef of the Year for *The Age Good Food Guide 2017*. I truly didn't see that coming and what great company I'm in, alongside so many chefs I admire and who I think should actually be Chef of the Year. I'm not sure I feel comfortable with it—I've been nominated before in previous years and I always feel like I don't deserve it—but especially not now, not yet, anyway. I mean, I'm struggling with the demons of being back in the kitchen and not even sure I still want to be there, so surely someone else deserves the award, someone confident in being a chef, let alone Chef of the Year.

It's a real Jekyll and Hyde moment. I feel so proud of the achievement, but at the same time a little embarrassed that I've been nominated. Chefs I admire, much better chefs, have won it before. For a moment I even let myself want it quietly, though I'm also completely content with the milestone of being nominated. These days though, these feelings come with thoughts of not deserving it. The attention, the awards—it's an evil balance.

Every chef has one, an asparagus dish that is. We wait forever for the little green, purple and white stalks to show their faces and for a few brief weeks they grace us with their presence before retreating and laying dormant until the next year.

I have been waiting for these guys to come into season to make this, the first dish to not involve the fire.

I start by carefully and lightly peeling the asparagus just to remove the thin outer layer, then I place them under a moist towel to avoid any chance of the stalks starting to dry out. A quick blanch in boiling water in groups of three for a three second count followed by a shock in salted ice water helps to keep them luminescent green.

I have a plan already for these guys. The thick stems will be dressed in buffalo milk from a herd of water buffalo three hours' south of the restaurant, then mixed with an earthy dill oil and laid underneath a pile of pungent spring herbs, with a fine grating of cured hen's yolk covering the stalks to finish. A clean, simple taste of spring.

11·09·2016

It's such a big room we are in, a hidden underground ballroom that I never knew existed, right in the heart of Melbourne.

It's nice to see so many familiar faces—industry folks. Some I've reconnected with over this past year and some I haven't seen for years. It's good to see everyone.

These parties are always fun, the glass of champagne that never ends, the too-salty finger food, the chefs, waiters and restaurant owners all dressed up. A rare night off, the hospitality night of nights.

8.30 pm

Did we just win that? Regional Restaurant of the Year, that's us right?

Yep, it says it right there on the giant screen—holy shit, we did win. IGNI is *The Age Good Food Guide 2017* Regional Restaurant of the Year.

9 pm

Please don't let it be me. Fuck it's me—yep, that's my name. FUCK, I've just been awarded Chef of the Year. Please don't make me say anything, just hand over the giant bottle of champagne and let me get off the stage. I find it so difficult being up here with everyone waiting for me to say something I know later I'll regret. I wish I could be better at these situations.

We have just won Regional Restaurant of the Year and Chef of the Year, and just like that Drew's phone lights up on alert for bookings. We watch it go crazy as one after the other they keep rolling in all night. It's as though someone has flicked a switch and turned on the lights.

We have achieved what I thought impossible. We have the attention, now what on earth do we do with it? I should be at my happiest, I've achieved a successful comeback, staked my flag firmly into the ground, yet I feel at my saddest—an intense loneliness. I have no idea why.

16·09·2016

I've finally got my hands on a few kilos of fresh snapper roe. I've been trying to find some for the last few weeks. I want to start to cure them before the weather starts to warm up,

I've done it plenty of times before, salted and hung them in a cool space to dry slowly. This time I want to try the same method but use the ambient warmth from the fire, letting the fresh roe catch a little of the residual smoke from the dying red gum. It's a gamble because the fire and smoke may produce too much heat and warm the roe sacks a little too much, sending them rancid. But it's worth a shot

I feel like we are controlling the fire much better these days, using less wood and charcoal.

Tonight is the *Time Out Magazine Awards*, the last of the hospitality award nights.

I'm not sure I've got my head around the recent awards let alone being nominated in *Time Out Magazine*. We have been fortunate enough to be nominated for a few very unexpected awards and again with some very good company.

Best Fine Dining

Chef of the Year

Restaurant of the Year

I feel more settled this time, less nervous in the environment and perhaps subconsciously with fewer expectations. I even manage to convince myself just to enjoy the night—it could be the last time that IGNI is acknowledged or even nominated, so enjoy it while it lasts.

It hits me, sitting at Tipo 00 sharing a late night post-awards meal with Jo, Drew and other friends from the industry. We just won Best Fine Dining and Chef of the Year, and not only did we win these awards but we have also managed somehow to clean sweep the awards season, being awarded and celebrated far more than I think we perhaps deserve at this stage of our restaurant's life.

I am proud of what we have all achieved but I also know what weight these awards carry. They are not to be taken lightly or with a grain of salt—we now have an expectation to not only live up to but also to exceed for every single guest who walks through our doors.

We have to analyse everything again from the start. Everything from the ease of our booking system and how we greet our guests to how we polish our plates and cutlery; everything from our glassware and rugs to our artwork, flowers and plants. But most of all we need to analyse how we treat each other. Are we respectful to one another? Are we supportive? Encouraging? Creative? Are we all happy? Because if we are and we have a culture that encompasses all of the fundamentals then we will be successful—we will exceed our guests' expectations because, simply put, happiness is contagious and is something genuine that cannot be faked. So, firstly, I have to allow myself to believe these awards are and were deserved and allow myself to say well done, congratulations, but now get back to work.

It's a moment of relief and satisfaction.

snacks

I love snacks. For me they provide the perfect way to settle into a meal and I can think of nothing better than being presented with a table with various elements on it to get everyone to start eating and talking. Given that at IGNI we have no menu, snacks also play an essential part in helping our front-of-house staff to break down any barriers between restaurant and guest quickly, which is why we serve them up as soon as we have had our initial conversation with a table and have ascertained their likes, dislikes and allergies. We tend to serve a selection of four to nine (though this has been up to eleven at one point) generous little bites that help to disarm and prepare for the meal ahead.

pickled mussels and zucchini flowers

500 g (1 lb 2 oz) mussels
55 g (2 oz) sugar
80 ml (2½ fl oz) rice vinegar
20 zucchini flowers, stems and stamens removed

Add the mussels to a large heavy-based saucepan together with 300 ml (10 fl oz) water. Cover with a lid, bring to the boil and cook for 2 minutes, then remove the mussels from the pan with a slotted spoon and plunge into ice-cold water.

Whisk the sugar and vinegar into the mussel cooking liquor in the pan while still warm to form a pickling liquid, adding more or less vinegar and sugar to get the right balance of sweet and sour. Add the mussel meat to the pickling liquid, discarding the shells, and refrigerate until needed.

Peel the zucchini flower petals back to open and place a mussel inside each, then fold back the petals to seal. Put the flowers on a hot grill briefly to crisp and char before serving.

dried beef

150 g (5½ oz) mushroom soy
150 g (5½ oz) sherry vinegar
40 g (1½ oz) grapeseed oil
1 teaspoon garam paste
200 g (7 oz) fatty hanger steak, cut into 5 mm (¼ in) slices

Mix all the wet ingredients together in a bowl with a whisk.

Lay the steak slices out on a tray and brush on both sides with the marinade. Refrigerate for 1 hour, then repeat the process twice more before placing the marinated steak slices onto dehydrator trays and drying out in a dehydrator on the highest setting for 4 hours, or until the beef is dry but still retains a little moisture from the fat. Store in an airtight container until needed.

roasted chicken skin with salted cod roe

You will need to use really fresh fish roe sacks here. You can use any fresh fish roe: cod, mullet, snapper or trevally work well. Make sure they are not damaged in any way and are free of blemishes.

> 100 g (3½ oz) soft white bread
> juice of 1 lemon
> 1 thinly sliced shallot
> 500 ml (17 fl oz) grapeseed oil
> dill, to garnish

salted cod roe

> salt
> 2 cod roe sacks
> olive oil

chicken skins

> 8 raw chicken skins

For the salted cod roe, start by filling a large bowl with a 10 per cent brine solution—that's 10 g (¼ oz) fine salt per 1 litre (34 fl oz/4 cups) of water. Once the salt has dissolved, carefully lower the roe sacks into the brine and leave to sit for 3 hours, then remove the sacks from the brine and pat dry with plenty of paper towel. Sprinkle a moderate amount of salt all over the roe sacks and leave at room temperature for 6 hours, or until the roe sacks have started to firm up.

When the sacks have started to firm, wipe as much salt off them as possible with a kitchen wipe then poke a hole in the top of each roe with a skewer and tie with a length of butcher's string forming a loop at one end. Leave to hang in a cool, drafty area to dry for 10–14 days. Lightly brush each roe sack with olive oil, wrap in plastic wrap and refrigerate until needed.

Soak the bread in a bowl with 400 ml (13½ fl oz) warm water until soft, about 20 minutes, then gently squeeze out the water and set aside. Blitz the bread, roe, lemon juice and shallot in a blender until smooth, then in a steady stream gradually pour in the grapeseed oil, adding a little warm water if the mixture becomes too thick. Season to taste with lemon juice and sea salt and refrigerate until needed.

For the chicken skins, remove all the excess fat and meat from the skin by scraping the underside carefully with a knife (be careful not to rip it). Spray a baking tray with oil and place the skins as flat as possible. Roast in a 200°C (400°F) oven for 25 minutes or until golden and crisp.

Remove the skins from the tray and place on absorbent towel to remove any excess fat. Spread liberally with cod roe and garnish with dill.

beetroot in aged duck fat/whey/mustard leaf

At IGNI we try not to put anything in the bin if we can help it and this includes anything that comes off the ducks we get in the restaurant, which are a staple on the menu. Because of the way they are raised (which is amazingly) the ducks are quite fatty, so we trim this fat off and keep rendering it down until we are left with a beautiful aged fat for cooking with.

Here we confit the beetroot slowly in the duck fat with a little sherry vinegar until they shrivel and develop a nice, jelly-like texture, then we put them over the grill to bring them up to temperature and lend them a little extra smokey flavour, which complements their sweet earthiness. The mustard leaf adds a little pepperiness to the dish without the need for seasoning and was the result of an experiment to see how much heat green leaves could withstand on the grill—I was amazed by how much they could take before they burnt.

2 beetroot (beets)
aged duck fat, for frying
splash of aged sherry vinegar
bunch of mustard leaves
clarified butter, for brushing

whey sauce

1 litre (34 fl oz/4 cups) acidic goat's whey
4 thyme sprigs
35 g (1¼ oz) comté, roughly chopped

serves 4

Peel the beetroot and use a ring cutter to cut into 5 cm (2 in) rounds. In a heavy-based saucepan, add enough duck fat to cover the base of the pan by 5 cm (2 in) and slowly heat until small bubbles start to appear. Slowly cook the beetroot in the aged duck fat, adding a splash of sherry vinegar, until they start to shrivel and become a jellied texture—this should take about 45 minutes. Set aside to cool.

Wash and clean the dirt from the mustard leaves. Cut out circles from the leaves using a ring cutter two sizes bigger than that used to cut the beetroot. Set aside.

For the whey sauce, add the whey and thyme to a heavy-based saucepan set over a low heat and slowly reduce to 500 ml (17 fl oz/2 cups). Remove half of the thyme. Blitz the mixture in a blender, adding the comté piece by piece, until smooth, then pass through a fine strainer.

To finish, warm the beetroot gently over a medium fire, being careful not to burn or crisp the undersides. Brush the mustard leaves with clarified butter and grill over a medium fire until the leaves begin to crisp. Plate as you wish.

october

I'm tired.

I know I'm not supposed to say that, but I am. It's been a long nine months. I know I'm meant to push and push, to carry on with all the bullshit bravado that comes with being a chef, the hours worked to be worn like a stupid badge of honour. I've been there, I've even perpetuated this very idea. But it's not how I wanted to do things this time. I want to do things differently than before, so I have to remember to do that and to actively go about making those changes. It's easy to fall into old bad habits, to make excuses and say that's just the way it's meant to be. But to find a balance of working hard and striving for something and also taking time to do other things, I've always struggled with that. It's always been one direction, full pace.

It's the hours it takes to get a restaurant open every day and for every service. It's the expectations I put on myself, let alone anyone else's. It's the not letting anyone down and always being better than the day before, in the little ways. How long did it take me to shell the peas yesterday, ten minutes? Today I will do it in eight. Or, I made the sauce for the fish at 9.15 yesterday, today I'll get it done by 9. All these are minutes saved in an effort to fit more jobs on the ever-increasing list.

I'm tired.

It's more mental than physical—I think. It usually is, but these days I'm not so sure.

I should feel comfortable enough to allow myself this tiredness, but I don't; rather, I question it.

'Come on, mate, push on, you've had plenty of sleep, four hours will do! Get on with it.'

It's nothing new for us cooks, getting sick and tired just isn't an option, it's simply out of the question. Plus there's a sense of pride and certainty that the place can't run without you, and truth be told it often can't. If you're not there to fillet the fish on your section, someone else has to; if you aren't there to watch dutifully as the stocks reduce to glossy sauces, someone else has to squeeze it in between their list of chopping bones and picking herbs; if you're sick you deal with it and in the process make everyone else in the kitchen sick with you. It's just the way it goes.

It's been a hectic nine months, and I've felt it every day and night; every hour of it has felt as if I've been holding my breath, keeping my body in a suspended state of tension and concern, trying to ignore the questions that keep forcing themselves in: 'What happens if this doesn't work? What happens if this place we have built and nurtured starts to collapse? What if the walls start to crumble with all of us inside?' The small comfort I'm taking now is that we are finally fully booked all six services for the foreseeable future. It's a mental and financial relief.

Lunch is just about to start, and I'm comfortable in our tiny office typing away on my computer, alone, a moment to stop and think. I do feel guilty that I'm not dealing with the beautiful honey that Helena has dropped off from her hives in East Geelong this morning, fresh with the sweet scent of wildflowers, nor am I putting to use the crisp, rigid, red-stalked celery Bruce has grown for us. I can't sit here long because after today's service we will be closed for the weekend and that celery will no longer be what it is today—hours out of the soil, firm, crunchy, juicy and sweetly bitter.

The dining room has started to fill with happy, excited guests, people coming to experience IGNI for the first time. It's showtime, I tell myself. Let's go.

12·10 pm

> I'm really uninspired at the moment. Maybe it's the weather. It's shit at the moment—rainy, windy, grey— but then again I guess that's spring in Victoria. Still, at least it's an excuse I can use to explain my mindset. Perhaps I'm just trying too hard. Either way, I hope it breaks soon because it's very frustrating.

04·10·2016

The honey bugs have started to come through the market—small bottom-dwelling ocean crustaceans known for their sweet meat. I've never really used them before and only eaten them on a few occasions. I've decided to order a few kilos to see how they go. If the texture is no good I'll make a sauce; if they turn out to be inspiring, with firm sweet flesh, then who knows where they will lead? A raw dish, perhaps. Fingers crossed they kickstart something.

I had such great plans today to spend some time in the kitchen alone and try out a few new ideas, specifically a spanner crab tart for a new snack—a tartlet made from mustard and parmesan with freshly picked crabmeat bound in an acidic emulsion. But I've woken up anxious, for no reason, really, or no reason I can recognise. Perhaps it's the looming deadline of this book that I have no idea how to write, perhaps it's the change of season or the constant need to change most of our dishes as the root vegetables are finished but the spring greens are yet to be any good. Whatever it is, it's all getting on top of me.

A holiday would be nice right about now. I've been keeping this diary, a daily snapshot of the year I opened IGNI, and it feels strange to be constantly writing about having no inspiration because I know (hope) it's still in there somewhere, trapped beneath these layers of self-doubt. I guess there's no other solution but to keep digging in the hopes of pulling something out.

05·10·2016

My body feels out of place, like three individual pieces that haven't been put together quite right, cold and disjointed, aching and stiff. I know what's coming next.

10 pm

I woke up this morning and felt as though the house had collapsed on me. Two storeys of rubble piled on top of me. I'm freezing cold despite the two t-shirts, flannel button-up and hooded jumper I must have wrestled on during the night, which all feel a bit damp, I'm guessing from the fever.

There's no choice for me not to go to work today. There is no one to take my place, no one to work my section while also watching out for all the little things throughout the day that make up the bigger things. Someday I'd like my restaurant to run without me, but it can't, not yet, not with the skeleton crew I run with every day.

I can't stop sneezing—one after another after another, my head pounding just a little more each time. And I can't taste anything, again, which is a bit of a worry. It's such an odd sensation when everything just tastes bitter or like nothing at all. How the hell am I going to season anything? It's hard just to keep standing up, and I know this is my body telling me to take a break. It's been on high alert for the past nine months since IGNI started.

Just for today, I'd like to go back to bed.

Some days are easier than others, and on days like today everything seems to flow. I still feel like shit, but my body is held upright thanks to a creative cocktail of drugs—some pharmaceutical, some natural—that are helping keep me focused. I still can't taste much at all, so fingers crossed the new dishes I'm about to serve to a couple of well-regarded food writers go well. The hungover dishwasher seems to like them, so here goes nothing.

> A few new dishes came together on the fly today with no real thought to them, just ingredients and produce we had on hand. They always seem to be born this way, but it's nerve-racking waiting for them to arrive, to feel like your own work is beyond your control and somehow at the mercy of the culinary gods. Inspiration can come at the oddest of times—a walk to work, a dream in the middle of the night, a passage in a book or in the shower mid-song. Or it can be the result of produce so good that your mind runs a million miles an hour with thoughts and ideas.

I'd forgotten that, how to just say, 'Fuck it, let's cook'. To find a service beat and rhythm that is different every day and cook our way through flavour and textures. It won't be perfect, it will never be free from mistakes the way they teach you to be, but it will be honest, it will be our moment of inspiration that we will share with the guests at IGNI.

I am determined today not to be scared anymore, scared of this defeating me. I won't hold back. I just want to cook, to create an intimate moment for our guests, one that is never repeated. I feel like it's all coming back to me, the reason I am doing this.

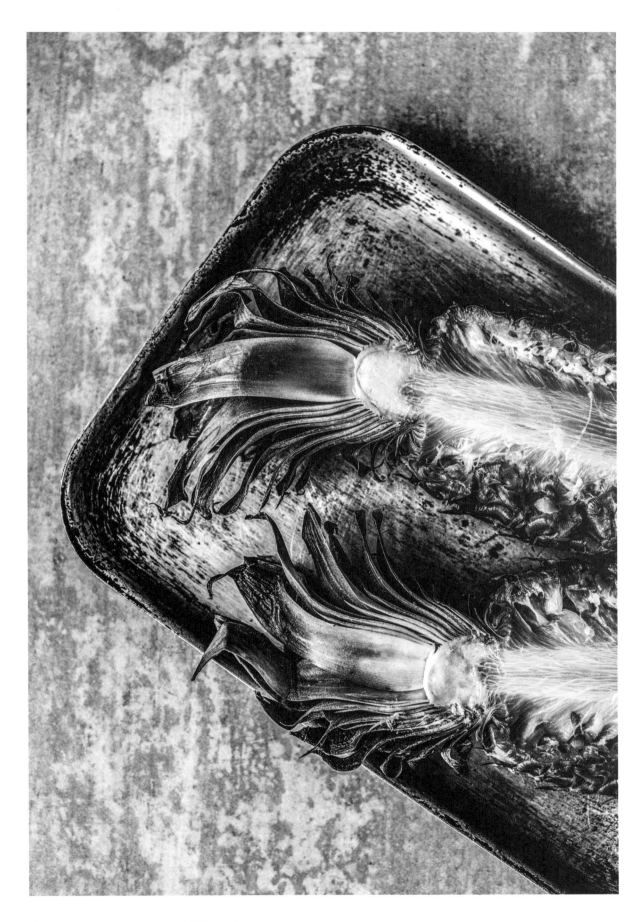

above: pineapple cooked overnight in coals

How quickly it can all change, though. Yesterday seemed so great despite being sick, today I seem to be getting worse with the flu. It's frustrating, and really I just want the week to be over.

A few dishes I liked from yesterday I'll serve again today, the results of just cooking and not trying to plan out every aspect of a dish, letting them instead be a reaction to the mood of the day. I try to convince myself to do this every day, but today I'm nervous about it.

spanner crab/smoked pork broth

aged duck/wet garlic/dried herbs

asparagus/egg yolk/spring herbs/buffalo milk

I can feel my mood slipping again. Perhaps it's being sick, or maybe it's the constant feeling of being caged here in the kitchen all the time. There is no space, nowhere to hide. IGNI is just a box with everything and everyone on show, just the bare bones of a restaurant, really.

It's the smallest of things, a dropped spoon or a broken glass, a frustrated sigh amplified a thousand times. There is simply nowhere to hide, and today I just want to run from it all.

Today is a day that will come and go, and I know nothing will get done. I won't do anything more than what is the bare minimum. It's a day when all my thoughts are foggy and static and I can't focus, and it's days like today where I find it difficult to feed myself, let alone anyone else, and it all seems too much.

I've come to accept that, for me, some days are just like this. It's frustrating beyond words, so I just keep to myself and stay as quiet as possible, but work goes on—it won't stop just because I'm feeling like this. It makes me feel guilty if I ignore the work too long; why should I feel like this, and what is compelling me to continue owning a restaurant or being a cook if I do?

If anyone were to read this they would probably want to slap me and tell me to get my shit together, and on some days I'd agree with them. I'd also tell them not to be deceived by the television-romance version of this industry; it's madness, at its core, and we are probably all mad for doing it.

I can't shake this flu and I'm struggling to stay awake. My body is launching a rather convincing argument to get me to slow down, but there's not much chance of that happening. I'm finding it hard to make some much-needed changes to the menu. The seasons are closing in and catching up on me; soon the last of the jerusalem artichokes will be done and I'm crossing my fingers the broad beans will be ready. But I can't really focus on any of that at the moment, because I'm just trying to stay awake. I probably should go to the doctor, but I won't. I hate doctors; they scare the living shit out of me—probably something to do with the chronic fear of dying I have—but anyway, on to bigger problems, I just burnt my sauce.

I've been trying to make this sauce for about an hour but every time I start it something happens to distract me—a question, a delivery, my phone ringing. When I finally get five seconds to concentrate on it

I burn it. Jesus, I'm convinced it's the induction's fault—such flat, direct heat. That's the excuse, anyway. The truth is I just keep fucking it up.

It's been happening a lot lately—little mistakes, little distractions. I have gotten pretty good at hiding them over the years but I hate making them; they embarrass me.

Perhaps it's the pressure of writing this book that's getting to me or maybe it's having the spotlight on us after winning the awards. I'm not sure.

Most days I feel like I'm waiting for something to break, waiting in vain for the cavalry to ride in and take charge.

Or maybe all of this is too good to be true and I'm just here biding my time, waiting for it to get fucked up again.

I don't think I've let myself feel comfortable yet, with any of it. It feels like the moment I do is the moment it will all go away again.

It's 5 pm Saturday and our dinner service starts in an hour. Currently we don't have nearly enough seafood; the planes that deliver our marron from Western Australia have been delayed, the winds too strong for take-off, while the day boats out fishing for snapper twenty minutes from the restaurant, the ones brave enough to face this weather, haven't returned yet.

I haven't seen weather like this—gale-force winds and the rain coming in sideways—in a long time. In fact, no one has. Almost everyone who has come through the doors today has said the same thing, what strange and unusual weather we are having.

At this stage I have six oysters, ten portions of fish, no marron, no crab, no scallops and no pippies, all crucial to the menu we have been running. The vegetables are yet another concern. No asparagus has arrived. I have a handful of peas left over from lunch and no more coming in today, the poly tunnels that grow our radishes and leaves have blown over, one of them even made it as far as the neighbour's paddock, so we don't have those ingredients either. And yes, we are fully booked.

> So here's the plan: let's just go for it, changing and adjusting the dishes we have on the fly. The garnish for the marron dish, pickles and pil pil, let's do it with the cured and smoked fish we have hanging from last week. We can run with ten portions of snapper; I'll just have to put a count on the running board. The pippies, well they are served with potato noodles cooked in roasted chicken fat and vinegar with a raw hen's egg on top, so let's just serve that without the pippies. Simple. Actually, wait... let's toss the noodles with dried black cabbage and horseradish instead.

It's somewhat stressful, but fun, too, these moments of spontaneous creation—dishes that will come and go with a service. It was once the reason I loved cooking so much.

spanner crab/smoked pork broth

I love to cook with spanner crab. Fishing for them depends on the weather, so they can come and go in terms of availability, but I am able to get them live and they have a good meat-to-shell ratio. The texture of the meat is good too and they have a lovely sweet flavour, which contrasts really well with the intense, sticky smoked pork broth here. Earth and sea at their best.

1 x 350–400 g (12½–14 oz) live spanner crab

smoked pork broth

3 brown onions, roughly chopped
4 carrots, roughly chopped
2 fennel bulbs, roughly chopped
6 garlic cloves, roughly chopped
100 ml (3½ fl oz) grapeseed oil
4 x 200 g (7 oz) smoked pork hocks
4 star anise
6 fresh bay leaves
10 coriander seeds
peel of 1 orange
5 litres (170 fl oz/20 cups) chicken stock

serves 4 with extra broth

For the smoked pork broth, sauté the onion, carrots, fennel and garlic in the oil in a deep heavy-based stockpot until the onions are translucent. Add the pork hocks and brown all over, then add the star anise, bay leaves, coriander seeds and orange peel and cook, stirring, until fragrant. Pour over the stock and 5 litres (170 fl oz/20 cups) cold water, bring to a simmer and cook for 6 hours over a low heat, skimming away any impurities that rise to the surface as you go. Remove the ham hocks from the broth and strip off the meat (keep this for using elsewhere). Pass the broth through a fine sieve, then return to the pan and keep warm.

Bring a large saucepan of water to a rapid boil, add the crab and cover with plastic wrap. Remove from the heat and leave to sit for 35 minutes, then remove the crab from the pan and leave to cool. Once cool, pick all the meat from the shell, being careful not to leave any behind. Set aside.

To serve, divide the crabmeat among deep serving bowls and spoon over the hot broth.

asparagus/egg yolk/spring herbs/buffalo milk

One for the short asparagus season.

8 asparagus spears
acidic herb leaves (such as sorrel, sheep sorrel or ice plant),
  to serve

egg yolks

300 g (10½ oz/11/3 cups) sugar
300 g (10½ oz) fine salt
4 egg yolks

dill oil

2 bunches dill, roughly chopped
100 ml (3½ fl oz) grapeseed oil

buffalo milk

150 g (5½ oz) buffalo yoghurt
juice of ½ lemon
pinch of white pepper

serves 4 with extra dill oil

For the egg yolks, combine the sugar and salt and mix well, then spread half the mix over the bottom of a plastic container in an even layer. Carefully lower the egg yolks onto the sugar and salt mixture, spoon over the remaining mix to cover completely and refrigerate for 3 days. Wash the yolks thoroughly in cold running water, pat dry and put into a dehydrator for 90 minutes or until dry and firm. Store in an airtight container until needed.

For the dill oil, add the dill and grapeseed oil to a blender and blitz together on high to form a bright-green oil. Strain through a fine sieve and chill in the freezer for 1 hour.

For the buffalo milk, mix the yoghurt, lemon and white pepper together in a bowl until smooth and runny. Set aside at room temperature until needed.

With a sharp peeler, lightly run down the length of the asparagus spears to remove a fine outer layer of skin. Add the asparagus to a large saucepan of water and blanch for 3 seconds before transferring to a bowl of ice-cold water to halt the cooking process.

To serve, arrange the asparagus spears on a plate. Season lightly with salt, dress with the buffalo milk and dill oil and grate over the yolk to cover the spears. Scatter over the herb leaves to finish.

aged duck/wet garlic/dried herbs

Duck is always on the menu at IGNI as the birds we receive from Greg and Jodi at Great Ocean Ducks are of a consistently exceptional standard. When the produce is as good as this, there's no need to try too hard or do much to it. Wet garlic is very young garlic that has yet to form into cloves and has a mild flavour, as opposed to the mature garlic we are used to seeing.

1 x 1.2 kg (2 lb 10 oz) good-quality duck, washed and
  thoroughly dried
300 ml (10 fl oz) reduced chicken stock
25 ml (¾ fl oz) tarragon vinegar
80 g (2¾ oz) clarified butter
1 bunch wet garlic, cleaned and washed

dried herbs

50 g (1¾ oz) cavolo nero (tuscan cabbage)
6 thyme sprigs
15 g (½ oz) lovage
15 g (½ oz) pepper leaves

serves 6

For the dried herbs, blanch the cavolo nero in a pot of boiling water and pat dry.

Roughly chop the cavolo nero and all the remaining ingredients and place everything in a dehydrator on a medium heat for 2 hours or until completely dried out. Leave to cool for 10 minutes, then transfer to a spice grinder and blitz together to a fine powder.

Wash the duck and pat dry, then remove the legs, head, wishbone and wings to leave the duck crown only, reserving the remainder for making a broth later. Set the duck crown over a medium red gum fire and roast until the skin crisps and turns golden brown. Turn the duck breast-side down onto a deep tray and leave to the side of the fire for 35 minutes or until cooked (the breast should feel firm but slightly yield to the touch). Remove the duck from the pan and set aside to rest.

Add the reduced chicken stock to the pan and bring to the boil, then simmer down for 6 minutes, or until reduced to a sauce-like consistency. Stir in the tarragon vinegar and keep warm.

Brush the clarified butter over the wet garlic and grill over hot (but not flaming) embers until charred and wilted.

To serve, divide the wet garlic among plates and dust with the dried herb powder. Slice the duck, arrange it next to the garlic and spoon over the sauce to finish.

november

I am failing to keep the promise to myself at the end of each week that I'll change the entire dish line-up on Thursday when we return, or that I'll spend Wednesday in the kitchen by myself working on ideas and thoughts. It never seems to work out that way. A million little things keep me distracted, and it's a constant disappointment to myself that causes me endless frustration. Why don't I just do it? What on earth could be stopping me from spending the days we are closed working on new ideas and techniques, tending to my scribbled notes from previous weeks? Mostly it's because come Sunday night I've had enough. Always feeling a little defeated by the week, I've usually had enough of cooking and just want a cold beer.

The frustration comes from feeling like we aren't—or I'm not—achieving anything. I know we are and I know we have; it's been a crazy year so far and I have it better than most chefs, I just feel like something's missing, something's not quite right.

The frustrating part is that it used to be so easy. Now, every idea or thought that I have, those moments of self-professed brilliance that flash in my mind for just a second, are dismissed, discarded as waste before they have even had a chance to escape and become anything, let alone dishes, sauces, desserts or garnishes.

It's a strange and scary feeling when you lose all faith in your ability. I feel like I'm drowning.

The voices in my head scream in chanting chorus, 'All creativity is lost, and we are doomed to fail.'

That's what it sounds like, the argument in my head.

The big problem I'm having is that I am relied on to work a section in the kitchen. Ideas float in and out of my head, but I never get time to explore any of them, like the dessert I wanted to sort out—flowering gum and fermented blueberries. I know it will work but I can't find the time to refine it. I've tried and failed at getting it done in between reducing sauces, filleting fish, picking herbs, writing a book, returning emails, negotiating new serviceware, oh, and running a whole separate business at the Hot Chicken Project.

I've slowly handed off jobs to Rowan and Jono, things I just can't get done. They don't seem to mind, slipping them into their already overloaded workloads.

I really need to sharpen my knives but there's no time for such luxuries, I tell myself, and get on with all the basic knifework needed to get my section ready for service—onions, carrots, leeks and bones cut for sauces, fish trimmed and portioned ready for roasting over the fire. I contemplate just buying new knives. That might be quicker and easier.

This time spent means I have very little time for anything else, only enough to help get the kitchen in shape for the coming service, to be a set of hands in the kitchen. It's something I used to enjoy but now a job I'm convinced is better left to someone else. The days pass quickly. We break down the kitchen order for the following day and then turn around to do lunch and dinner services back to back, our days on repeat. Before I know it it's the end of the week and I've gotten nothing else done, I've achieved nothing to move the restaurant forward, instead I feel like I've only managed to keep it running. I know we need to do more than that if we want to become the restaurant we all want to be.

I do have a solution for the day-to-day work that is taking up too much of my time. I've asked a chef who helped me at the end of Loam to come home and take up a position here. He's been working his way through Scandinavia for the past three years, so what an arsehole he must have thought I was when I called and said to him, 'Hey, wanna leave working and learning from some of the best restaurants and chefs in the world, in the hottest place for food right now, and move back to Geelong instead? To work in a restaurant that has no idea what it's doing, with me, a guy who is collapsing under the weight of self-doubt?'

Somehow I must have sold it better than that because he agreed to come back.

This, I hope, will give IGNI the push it needs to keep progressing, and to push it further, to be a better version of what it has already become.

opposite: roasted chicken skin with salted cod roe (page 191)

above: broccoli heart/macadamia/cabbage oil (page 177)

11·11·2016

7 am

Everyone is exhausted. No one is complaining but I can see it in their faces. Their movements are slower and less economical than a few months ago, or even a few weeks ago. Small mistakes are being made. Our eyes are not as bright as when we started this journey. IGNI, without a doubt, is on autopilot, hanging in the air hoping not to crash land before the Christmas break. There is little doubt we are all burnt out, or maybe it's just me. I hate the monotony of these fifteen-hour days, running in circles—clean, cook, clean, cook. I need a break from the repetition of kitchen life.

20·11·2016

I always seem to find out important news via text, and this time it comes from our accountant, Scott, at 6 am. 'Only three to go,' he says.

The *Herald Sun* has released its Top 100 Victorian Restaurants list for 2016 and we are number four, and winner of Best New Restaurant. Number four, holy shit!

I can't believe the company we have been considered in, up there on the top of the same list with Attica and Brae. I feel so grateful that we have even been considered.

It's finally warm out, the morning sun golden. Today is a good day.

25·11·2016

There's a weird vibe in the restaurant today, but I can't really be bothered trying to figure it out. Usually something like this bugs me and I pry and prod to find out where the issue or issues are, but today I'm just here to tick off the week in the hope of getting to the end sooner. Most, if not all, creativity has ceased to exist within any of us. I have beautiful prawns fresh from the Clarence River in the cool room, with no idea what I'll do with them.

Previously I've served them raw with milk, dill oil and frozen rhubarb, and people loved them, but it sounds like a terrible idea now.

Maybe I could grill them quickly over the fire and then toss them in a vinegar I can make from their head juices... then perhaps after everyone has left I'll run that head-juice vinegar through a rough-cut semolina pasta and grate parmesan over it until you can't see any pasta anymore, just the bright red juices from the prawns.

Perhaps the answer is that I don't want to cook like I have before, or like everyone is expecting me to; maybe it's passed me by.

Two new dishes came out of the push to get ready for service today. We had a regular in for lunch and this will be his third visit in as many weeks. I missed his name on the running sheet this morning—I read through it pre-coffee and nothing stuck with me.

It's 11.20, and he has a 12.30 booking.

I have some blueberries I've fermented in goat's whey. They have the texture of raisins, with an intense fruit sweetness, and they have become quite chewy. I like them, and I'm happy with how they have turned out.

> We have also been working on an ice cream made from flowering gum, a native eucalyptus. I've been walking past a tree on the way to work always grabbing a leaf and rubbing it between my palms—there's something comforting about the smell. We haven't really gotten it right yet, it's either been too sweet or the flavour from the infusion has fallen over during the freezing process, but on the fifth try this morning I think we finally have it right. Something I can use.

fermented blueberries/flowering gum

One new dish for our regular, now what else do we have floating around the kitchen?

I still have the prawns, so I'll just try the dish I've been thinking about—par-cooking them over hot burning charcoal just enough to char the outsides but still leave them mostly raw, then slicing them thinly. I've made a vinegar from all the head juices and fresh bay leaf which I'll use to dress the meat, finished off with a thickened broth of tamarind and black russian tomato—acidic, sweet and sour. Bruce has dropped off a bag of fragrant coriander blossoms, I'll use them to finish.

clarence river prawn/tamarind and tomato

whey ferment

I've been working with a local goat dairy for the past twelve years or so, ever since they started. At first I asked for their milk (which they weren't selling at the time and which has since won gold at the Melbourne show) and then later their left-over whey from the cheese-making process, which puzzled them until I explained what I was doing with it. We've made lots of stuff together since and it's these relationships with our suppliers that make IGNI the restaurant that it is.

This is a great starter for fermenting vegetables, leaves and roots. After the fermentation has taken place it can also be used as a base liquid for cooking vegetables and grains or as a seasoning for sauces.

4 litres (135 fl oz/16 cups) acidic goat's whey
8 tablespoons fine salt

makes 8 litres (270 fl oz/32 cups)

Combine the ingredients and 4 litres (135 fl oz/16 cups) water in a very clean bucket or container and stir until the salt has dissolved.

At this stage, add your chosen ingredients for fermenting, being sure to submerge them fully, then cover the container with muslin and leave it to sit at room temperature. Depending on the ambient temperature of the room, the fermenting process can take anywhere from 7 days to 3–4 weeks. Once fermentation has taken place, drain off the liquid into another clean container to use again, and store your fermented ingredients in an airtight container or sterilised jar until needed.

cultured buttermilk sorbet

This is best as an accompaniment to stewed seasonal fruits.

415 g (14½ oz) cultured buttermilk
200 g (7 oz) glucose
1 egg white

serves 4

Add the buttermilk and glucose to a blender and blitz together, then add the egg white and blitz until combined. Strain, then add to an ice-cream maker and churn until frozen.

above: fresh cheese after being hung over the fire

clarence river prawn/tamarind and tomato

I don't tend to use prawns all that much as I find it hard to get them in any decent condition, but one day my fish guy at Clamms Seafood rang me up and told me he'd got his hands on some really good ones. I told him to send me a kilo. When they turned up and they were as good as he said I knew they'd make the perfect match for this tamarind and tomato combo I'd had kicking around for a while.

In the restaurant we charred the prawns briefly over the coals and served them with coriander blossoms and a vinegar made from the prawn head juices, but they work just as well served raw like this with a sprinkle of this seaweed salt, which is a great seasoning for any fish or shellfish.

150 g (5½ oz) tamarind pulp
2 kg (4 lb 6 oz) over-ripe black Russian tomatoes
15 g (½ oz) salt flakes
6 large clarence river prawns
assorted mustard leaves, to garnish

dried seaweed salt

100 g (3½ oz) dried sea lettuce
45 g (1½ oz) salt flakes

serves 6

Put the tamarind pulp in a bowl, cover with 200 ml (7 fl oz) boiling water and leave to cool to room temperature.

Roughly chop the tomatoes and add to a bowl. Sprinkle over the salt and let sit for 30 minutes, then transfer to a blender with the tamarind pulp and water and blend together on high for 3 minutes. Pour the mixture into a sieve lined with muslin, cover with plastic wrap and set over a bowl in the fridge to pass through slowly—the broth will run clear.

For the dried seaweed salt, add the sea lettuce and salt flakes to a spice grinder and blitz together to form a powder.

Prepare the prawns by lightly washing in cold water, peeling away the shells and heads and carefully removing the intestines with a small toothpick, piercing the flesh and lifting them out. Trim away any excess flesh and slice thinly.

To serve, arrange the prawns in a deep bowl in a single layer, sprinkle over a little of the seaweed salt and garnish with mustard leaves. Pour over the broth at the table to finish.

fermented blueberries/flowering gum

Another ice cream. But why not? I think as chefs we can often get too tricky when it comes to dessert and in doing so use a lot of emulsifiers and gelatins that can weigh heavily on the diner, leaving you to digest a lot of what are—essentially—gluing agents. I'd much rather have something simple, clean and fresh like ice cream instead.

This one took me a while to get right. After some tweaking we served it first to a regular but I was still unsure of it. It only got its place on the menu when the kitchen crew from Embla came around, tried it, went mad for it and asked for seconds, so I just sent the whole tub I had prepared. We now serve it with Davidson plum and pine needle yoghurt, using the fermented blueberries instead in a petit four.

freeze-dried blueberry powder, to serve

fermented blueberries

1 litre (34 fl oz/4 cups) acidic goat's whey
pinch of salt flakes
pinch of sugar
1 tablespoon raw honey
500 g (1 lb 2 oz) blueberries, washed in filtered water
Ultra-Tex 4 starch powder

flowering gum ice cream

275 g (9½ oz) goat's milk
250 g (9 oz) jersey cream
100 g (3½ oz) flowering gum leaves
7 egg yolks
220 g (8 oz/1 cup) sugar

serves 4 with extra blueberries

Mix the whey, salt, sugar and honey, and whisk to dissolve the ingredients. Add the mixture to a vacuum bag together with the blueberries and seal for 5 seconds. Leave to sit at room temperature for 3 days or until the berries have fermented (they'll have a light fizz to them and will have started to shrivel). Transfer to a non-reactive container and place in the fridge.

For the ice cream, warm the milk, cream and gum leaves in a saucepan to 85°C (185°F). Whisk the yolks and sugar together until pale and fluffy. Slowly temper the warm milk mixture into the eggs, whisking to combine. Transfer the mixture to a blender and blitz for 10 seconds, then strain and chill before pouring into an ice cream machine and churning until frozen.

Strain the liquid from the blueberries and thicken with ultra-tex 4 to pouring consistency (you'll need to add about 2 per cent of the liquid weight). Pour the liquid over the berries and return to room temperature.

To serve, add a tablespoon of the blueberries and liquid to the centre of four shallow serving bowls. Top each with a spoonful of ice cream and dust with a little freeze-dried blueberry powder to finish.

december

We are trying to figure out how to afford more staff. Not an easy equation when you only have a thirty-seat restaurant, but we do need two more for longevity, one in the kitchen and one on the floor, full time. So once again it's back to the puzzle of how to grow our little restaurant to make it better and better, although I do wonder if it's just me that needs to be better.

> I keep asking myself the same question: how do we make what we do better, each service better than the last, how do we make what we do more refined?

The quick, short answer is more hands, more hours of labour, more time to focus on attention to detail, but to do that we need to manage our time a little better than we have been, to put the foot back on the accelerator. It all takes energy and that's something I know I don't have in abundance right now.

05·12·2016

Today by chance a couple of heavy hitters have fallen in our lap. Let's call it fortuitous timing, or luck, or perhaps a little clever persuasion—definitely a sales pitch and some pleading—but they have agreed to leave their comfortable jobs and lives at restaurants at the top of their game to join us in Victoria's second city. They have agreed to come aboard the good ship IGNI.

This comes as somewhat of a relief, I think, for everyone. The survival game we have been playing will come to an end. We will have fresh eyes, thoughts and motivations. I'm looking forward to taking stock.

14·12·2016

I wish the weather would hurry up and stay warm, or even warm up at all. It's been the coldest start to summer I think I can remember, grey and overcast. It really doesn't do much for anyone's mood after such a long, cold winter for this part of the world.

I need it to stay hot to give the berries a chance to ripen properly. I always like having a berry dessert on during the season and sometimes longer if we have managed to have excess to ferment, preserve or purée and freeze. To me berries are the perfect dessert, a sweetness balanced by a burst of acid. I currently have a curious obsession with the aroma of fresh bay leaf and raspberries, and I'm just waiting for them to ripen. I know that however the combination works out, it will need lemon in there somewhere or maybe I should just wait to see how the season pans out. If the raspberries don't ripen to their fullest, or at all, they will stay firm and sour.

The thought has crossed my mind to get some raspberries delivered. It is tempting, but ultimately I know they will be underripe and cold stored and I inevitably will be disappointed, so I don't. Instead I just sit with the anticipation and excitement for the season. It's quite nice really, it brings a smile to my face.

I've also been reading about lacto-fermented berries for the coming season, using raw honey and whey to kick off the ferment. I immediately charge through loose ideas of duck smoked over apple wood, using the sourness and sweetness of the berries to offset the duck's richness.

I must remember to pick some fresh bay leaf tomorrow, there is a tree right outside my living room window.

Today we started drying all the king george whiting and baby snapper frames left over from a dish, high enough above the fire to remove them from any direct heat and allow the frames to dry but not cook. I'm leaving half, after a quick wash in saltwater, to dry naturally, others I've brushed with sesame oil or miso to use later in broths and sauces, or ground into a powder for a seasoning on vegetables. It's opening up a new world of possibilities; bones, and leftovers too big for the dehydrator, we can dry slowly and successfully by using the ambient heat of the fire to do the work and along the way impart subtle smoke from the slowly burning red gum embers. It's probably something done a thousand times before but something until now I've never given any thought to. I've just been too busy getting through the day, surviving the service, stuck in the perpetual motion of the day-to-day.

I've ditched the raspberry and bay leaf idea as I seem to be doing with most things these days. I have no confidence that any of my ideas are any good. Even if I get to the stage of actually making them I question whether they taste anywhere near to decent. I also keep forgetting to pick the bay leaf as I leave my house half awake each morning. I might come back to it, but, like most things, I'm not sure yet.

There is a familiar smell in the air that I've started to notice on the still nights and early mornings on the walk to work. It's a comforting smell, one that reminds me of playing in the countryside as a kid, the smell in the air after a summer rain, a damp wet heat releasing all the aromas of the natives growing wild. It's a unique smell, one that is burnt into my memory.

I've started casually grabbing leaves off all the different trees, rubbing them between my palms to release the essential oils and try to figure out exactly which one has such an impact on my memory. There are scents of lemon, freshly mowed grass and deep heat.

> I've started to walk a little slower home each night. It's not far, twenty minutes maybe, but it's giving me time to unwind and clear my head. A funny thing happens when you give yourself a little space and time. If you let yourself slow down just a little you notice all the things you failed to see when rushed.

You notice the smells of the neighbourhood gardens in summer bloom, lemon and lime, pepper from old pepper trees planted on every corner, the smell of roses standing tall in perfectly curated gardens, stems as thick as old grape vines. It makes me feel more connected to the space, to see it as a living place, not just a concrete jungle.

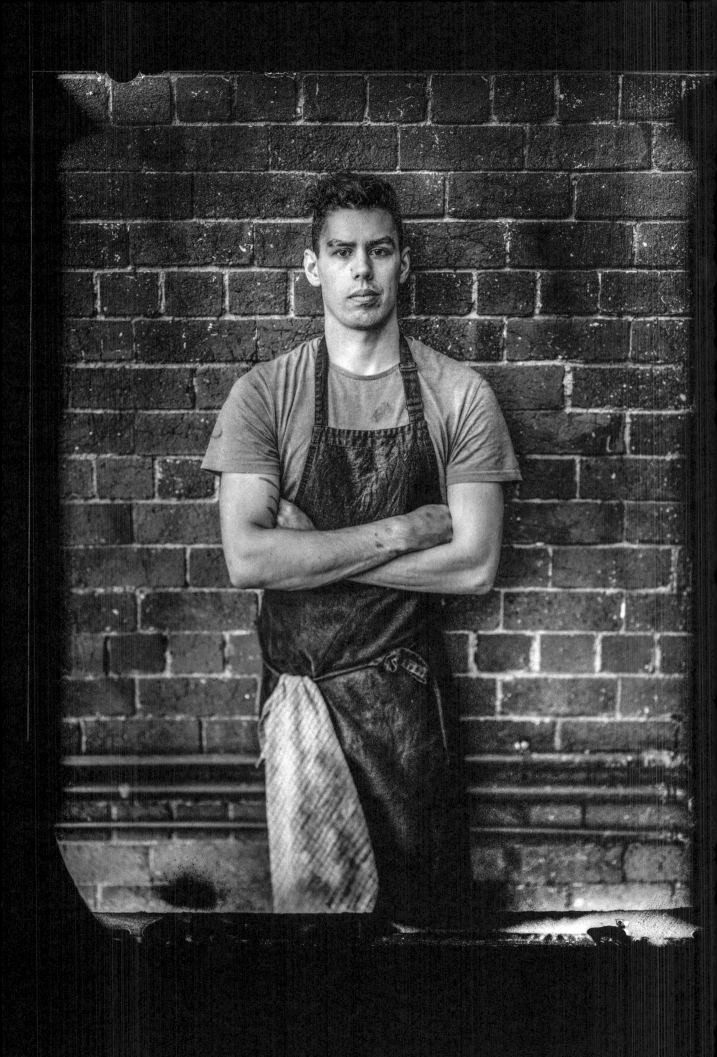

dried fish bone broth/salted plums/herbs

While I love the idea of this dish, this is something that I tried which I felt didn't quite work—despite being very happy with both elements, the balance between the massive flavours of the fish broth and the salted plums seemed to be just that bit too severe. Perhaps I just wasn't in the right headspace at the time to be happy with it, though, as everyone else who tried it seemed to really like it.

aromatic herbs, to serve

salted plums

1 bunch purple shiso, leaves picked
2 tablespoons rock salt
250 g (9 oz) greengage plums

dried fish bone broth

2 medium-sized dried fish skeletons
50 g (1¾ oz) fish skin
1 fresh bay leaf
4 peppercorns
1 small piece of dried kelp
½ teaspoon white miso paste
500 ml (17 fl oz/2 cups) chicken stock
1 tablespoon mushroom soy
1 tablespoon mirin
pinch of salt

serves 4–6

For the salted plums, place the shiso leaves in a blender with the rock salt. Pulse briefly to form a sand-like texture (don't run the blender continuously as the salt will become wet and mushy).

Gently squeeze the plums to break the skins. Arrange the plums on a large tray, sprinkle over the salt and roll around to coat well. Cover and leave to sit at room temperature for 24 hours.

The next day, lightly wash the plums and tear the cheeks from the stones. Place the plum cheeks in a dehydrator over a low heat overnight, then store in an airtight container until needed.

For the dried fish bone broth, add the fish bones, fish skin, bay leaf, peppercorns, kelp, miso and chicken stock with 200 ml (7 fl oz) water and bring to a gentle simmer. Cook gently for 45 minutes, skimming the impurities from the surface of the broth as you go.

Strain the broth and return it to the pan, then bring to a simmer and reduce by a third. Stir in the mushroom soy, mirin and salt and keep warm.

To serve, place six of the salted plum cheeks in a bowl and scatter over your choice of aromatic herbs (I like to use baby basil and lime- and lemon-scented herbs). Pour over 100 ml (3½ fl oz) of broth and repeat with the remaining bowls.

above: salted blue eye skeleton

10-year-old dairy cow/dandelion/kidney fat sauce

Like most of what we do at IGNI this recipe is simple, but relies on great produce. We were lucky enough to be able to share one of our shiitake grower's retired milkers, but if you can't get your hands on this kind of produce, a well-aged piece of beef will do. A good butcher should have kidney fat readily available. Pick red dandelion just as it is going to seed—the leaves will handle the fire a lot better and will give you a nice, chewy texture.

1 x 200 g (7 oz) 10-year-old dairy cow rump steak
 (or well-aged rump steak)
salt flakes
clarified butter
1 bunch red dandelion
juice of 1 lemon

kidney fat sauce

100 ml (3½ fl oz) grapeseed oil
2 brown onions, roughly chopped
6 carrots, roughly chopped
200 g (7 oz) kidney fat, diced
2 litres (68 fl oz/8 cups) brown chicken stock
aged apple-cider vinegar, to taste

serves 2

For the kidney fat sauce, heat the grapeseed oil in a heavy-based saucepan, add the onion and carrots and sauté over a low heat until softened but not coloured. Add the diced kidney fat and render slowly, then pour over the chicken stock, bring to a simmer and cook for 30 minutes. Strain and return to the pan and continue to simmer until reduced by a third. Add a splash of vinegar to cut the richness, to taste, and keep warm until needed.

Bring the rump steak to room temperature, season with salt and brush with clarified butter. Roast the steak over a medium fire, moving it often around the flames and turning occasionally, until the surface is caramelised. Remove from the heat and leave to rest on a wire rack in a warm place.

Brush the dandelion leaves with clarified butter and season with salt, then grill them over a high flame until they wilt and just begin to char. Squeeze over the lemon juice and remove from the heat.

Plate as you wish.

january

10·01·2017

We are back, fully booked, ready to go and rested. Well, some of us are—I seemed to have spent my time off in a steady state of anxiety about the coming year. It's tiring having your mind looped on one thing, always thinking of how to do better, nit picking the faults of what you do and how you do it, analysing every aspect of your days, weeks and months.

I do remember making myself a promise to change this—the way I am—but it's just my nature I guess, and is proving difficult to change.

20·01·2017

One year ago today we opened the doors at IGNI. It's 365 days since I was a nervous wreck throwing up in the shower wondering why I was about to open a restaurant at all. 365 days since I lay in bed, covers pulled over my head, hoping the whole world would just disappear, praying I didn't have to face opening day.

But it's also 365 days since I managed to get myself out of bed, put on a brave face and say, 'Fuck it, what's the worst that could happen, I already can't stand the thought of cooking, so what if I fall back in love with it all? Would that really be a bad thing?'

It's 365 days since we welcomed our first guests through the doors, filled the dining room with smoke, held our breath, threw caution to the wind and said, 'Fuck it all, here goes nothing.'

At times it feels as though the year has passed in a flash, a single moment. I can't even recall it at times, it's just a fragmented memory through a distorted rearview mirror. A year that somehow just vanished into thin air, the only evidence left being these pages.

Over this time I've beaten myself black and blue over the smallest of failures, buried the joys of success with a nagging feeling that I should be doing better, or maybe that I shouldn't be doing this at all. Some days I've held on just long enough to finish the day then collapsed on the couch silent with frustration, caught in a spiral of never-ending thoughts of negative moments. It's a space I've felt most comfortable in, a space I've trained myself to live in.

The whole idea of opening a restaurant, this homecoming of sorts, has been a difficult one, and that's without mentioning this process of writing it all down. Exposing myself on these pages has been like being forced to stand naked in front of a mirror and then seeing all the imperfections, the lumps and bumps, the ones we all can't stand to look at. Life's battle scars. It has been as honest as I could allow myself to be as a person and as a cook. It's not been a comfortable story to tell but it's one I'd committed to telling—self-therapy, of sorts.

It seems a world away from today. Today there is a clarity, even a comfortable relationship with the fire and with cooking. I feel there is also a certain calmness within the energy of the restaurant—our space and relationship has become comfortable, well seasoned. A year has passed and we know how to exist with each other. With our successes and failures we have been through almost every emotion possible and a story now exists within these walls, they now carry a life of their own.

There was a moment during a fleeting conversation with a guest recently that resonated with me—a simple throwaway sentence, spoken with a smile as they were walking out the door and into the alleyway, which stopped me in my tracks. It was as if the rest of the room fell silent and everyone around me became statues, a sentence that stuck in my head for the rest of the night and for weeks to come.

'Chef, thank you for cooking for me.'

An instant flash of recognition. Why had I been causing myself all this anguish and grief? This affected hatred I had towards cooking was stifling any chance of my moving beyond those barriers. It was a weight I needed to let go of, if I didn't, I would never be able to let myself enjoy the freedom of simply just cooking.

Now, I'm not sure this was how it was intended. Perhaps it was just a transaction of politeness or perhaps they were genuinely thankful for the experience but I spent a lot of time with those words echoing. What exactly was it they were thankful for? Was it the act of cooking, the transaction between cook and guest? Or something more? Regardless, it was the moment I was finally ready to hear something other than the noise in my own head.

Twelve months on and the days at the restaurant have more rhythm. We are better cooks. I'm a better cook. The swarming mist of anxiety has lifted, the path to creativity seems clearer, the weight of self-expectation and criticism has diminished, well, is at healthier levels at least. I see the day more clearly. I don't feel trapped, or overwhelmed. I am no longer scared to fail. A burnt sauce is now just a burnt sauce—it happens.

What we do at IGNI is not hard. We are not the best cooks but what we do is look for what we think is the most interesting angle on it all. A smoked duck can, on the day, quickly become a pickled and smoked duck—we approach our food from left field, upside down and inside out (and we fail more than we succeed), but above all we cook simply with a 'let's see what happens' attitude. There are no recipes as such and no formal plan for the week, just produce arriving after discussions with our farmers and suppliers. We light the fire and see where it takes us—an increasingly diminishing skill in a food world so reliant on perfection. We live and die by each service, each piece of meat, warmed sauce or picked herb. Everything is caught in a moment, each plate a little different to the last, each conversation at the table unique—an interaction with our guests that if we don't get right we will never get back. Our days are spent in a series of vanishing moments—polishing glasses, plates and silverware, reducing sauces, butchery, service and cleaning—constantly trying to hit the mark, to get it right in ever-changing conditions.

Has my love of cooking returned? That's a difficult question to answer. My relationship with it is different; how could it not be? I suppose at first I expected it to be the same—deep down I wanted that hunger I knew so well to return. But it's a little more arms' length now rather than headfirst in love; let's call it romantically cautious. I am... wary, careful not to let it consume all aspects of my life but at the same time letting it take little parts. Just enough. Because, simply, that is what it demands, that is the nature of it all—this chosen life as a cook.

Aaron Turner

Growing up by the coast in Portland, Victoria, Aaron studied graphic design before travelling and working overseas. In 2009 he opened his first restaurant, Loam, in Drysdale, which went on to win numerous awards including Regional Restaurant of the Year in *The Age Good Food Guide 2012* and Regional Restaurant of the Year in *Gourmet Traveller*. Since closing Loam in 2013 Aaron has worked and consulted in Nashville and opened The Hot Chicken Project and IGNI in Geelong. In its first year of business IGNI has won *Gourmet Traveller*'s Restaurant of the Year and has been awarded two hats by *The Age Good Food Guide 2016*, as well as winning the guide's awards for both Regional Restaurant of the Year and Chef of the Year.

Julian Kingma

Julian started his photography career at *The Herald* in 1988 as a cadet. Since going freelance after 10 years as Head Features Photographer for *The Sunday Age*, he has worked for various national and international publications including *Gourmet Traveller*, *Condé Nast Traveller*, *Harper's Bazaar* and *Rolling Stone*. Julian has won Quill Awards for Best Portrait and Best Picture Story, Australian Nikon Photographer of the Year and has exhibited at the National Portrait Gallery in Canberra. He is at his happiest bobbing around on his surfboard in the early hours at Bells Beach, Victoria, near his home on the Surf Coast.

To Mum, Reinhard and Genaya for always having my back. Thank you.

To Jo and Drew for being the best front-of-house team, business partners and friends anyone could hope for.

To Nancy for making my messed-up head and words make sense. For editing the edits, finding better words for my swear words and suggesting better ways to write delicately without telling me I was wrong (even though most of the time I was).

To Rowan and Jono for being great cooks and even greater people.

To Jane for understanding why I wanted to write this book and having the blind faith that I could actually get the job done.

To Julian. I couldn't think of a better person to shoot this story—thank you.

And lastly to Merryn, Gareth, James and Blake for coming aboard the good ship IGNI.

Julian Kingma would like to thank:

Jason Lee, Troy Bradford and Allen Crooks for all their inspiration, help and encouragement in all things film and expired polaroid.

New 55 for the film stock.

My wife Marijke for scrounging the net for old plates and cutlery.

And a huge thank you to my collaborator in crime—Aaron Turner—for having me on board and making this book such an amazing project to work on. I will be forever grateful for your kindness, friendship, patience and trust.

Published in 2017 by Hardie Grant Books, an imprint of
Hardie Grant Publishing

Hardie Grant Books (Melbourne)
Building 1, 658 Church Street
Richmond, Victoria 3121
hardiegrantbooks.com

Hardie Grant Books (London)
5th & 6th Floors
52–54 Southwark Street
London SE1 1UN
hardiegrantbooks.com

The publisher would like to thank Anna-Marie Wallace at Made OF Australia
for allowing us to reproduce a pattern from her ceramics on the cover.

A Cataloguing-in-Publication entry is available from the catalogue of
the National Library of Australia at www.nla.gov.au

Igni
ISBN 978 1 74379 265 0

Publishing Director: Jane Willson
Managing Editor: Marg Bowman
Editor: Simon Davis
Designer: Vaughan Mossop
Photographer: Julian Kingma
Production Manager: Todd Rechner
Production Coordinator: Rebecca Bryson

Colour reproduction by Splitting Image Colour Studio
Printed and bound in China by 1010 Printing International Limited